At the age of nineteen, **Kenny McGovern** was diagnosed with 'social anxiety disorder' and eventually became too ill to carry on working. As the years passed, he became almost housebound as a result of his illness and as such lost touch with many parts of life that, although enjoyable, are often taken for granted. Simple pleasures such as buying a nice sandwich from a local café or going out for a meal became impossible for him to do.

As a result of this, and because of his love of food and cooking, he eventually took to trying to recreate many of his favourite shop-bought foods at home. 'If I can't go to McDonald's, I'll make my own,' was his philosophy. Over a period of five years or more he tested and tweaked many, many recipes, his new hobby quickly building into an obsession.

In 2010, Kenny decided to publish some selected recipes in his first book, *The Takeaway Secret*. It became an instant bestseller following word-of-mouth recommendations on the internet.

With huge support and encouragement from readers, his confidence grew, along with his food obsession. As a result, Kenny once more ventured out into the world, researching and learning about the historic links between street food and local people, and the recent upsurge in the modern, exciting and vibrant street-food culture. His next book, *The Street Food Secret*, was released in 2017, followed by *The American Diner Secret* in 2019, *The Indian Takeaway Secret* in 2021, *The Chinese Takeaway Secret* in 2022 and *The Mexican Takeaway Secret* in 2023.

Kenny's passion for recreating delicious takeaway, restaurant and street food-style dishes remains as strong as ever!

T0300756

ALSO BY KENNY MCGOVERN

The Takeaway Secret

More Takeaway Secrets

The Street Food Secret

The Takeaway Secret (2nd edition)

The American Diner Secret

The Indian Takeaway Secret

The Chinese Takeaway Secret

The Mexican Takeaway Secret

THE THAI TAKEAWAY SECRET

How to Cook Your Favourite
Fakeaway Dishes at Home

Kenny McGovern

ROBINSON

ROBINSON

First published in Great Britain in 2024 by Robinson

1 3 5 7 9 10 8 6 4 2

A CIP catalogue record for this book
is available from the British Library.

ISBN: 978-1-47214-824-7

Typeset in New Caledonia by Hewer Text UK Ltd, Edinburgh
Printed and bound in Great Britain by Clays Ltd, Elcograf S.p.A.

Papers used by Robinson are from well-managed forests and other responsible sources.

Robinson
An imprint of
Little, Brown Book Group
Carmelite House
50 Victoria Embankment
London EC4Y 0DZ

An Hachette UK Company
www.hachette.co.uk

www.littlebrown.co.uk

How To Books are published by Robinson, an imprint of Little, Brown Book
Group. We welcome proposals from authors who have first-hand experience
of their subjects. Please set out the aims of your book, its target market
and its suggested contents in an email to howto@littlebrown.co.uk

NOTES ON THE RECIPES

Throughout this book you'll find many recipes that call for light chicken stock. You can make your own by following the recipe on page 191, or use any good-quality unsalted or low-salt chicken stock. If the stock you have is salty, dilute it with an equal amount of water, or adjust salt levels in your chosen recipe to suit.

Eggs used throughout the book are medium-sized eggs, unless specified otherwise.

Any neutral-flavoured vegetable oil may be used (I typically use sunflower oil).

Thai soy sauce can be thought of in a similar way to Chinese soy sauces, but the flavour is noticeably different so it's worth sourcing Thai brands (I like the Healthy Boy brand) for these recipes. Thin soy sauce adds a salty flavour for seasoning, thick soy sauce adds colour with a touch of sweetness and sweet soy sauce adds a more specific sweet note. You can think of thin soy sauce in a similar way to light soy, and thick soy sauce in a similar way to dark soy. Sweet soy sauce is thick and syrupy and adds a delicious note to stir-fried noodle dishes.

Making curry pastes is good fun, but shop-
bought curry pastes are more than acceptable.
I like Mae Ploy brand curry pastes.

When purchasing spices, try not to buy more than you
need for the immediate future – fresh spices will add
great flavour to your dishes, while older spices will
lose some of their flavour and aroma over time.

Coconut milk is an essential ingredient in Thai cooking
– try to find good-quality brands with a high coconut
percentage in the ingredients list. Aroy-D brand is good.

Good-quality jasmine rice is deliciously fragrant. Royal
Umbrella and Green Dragon brands are good.

CONTENTS

Introduction   1
Equipment   3
Store-cupboard ingredients   11
Fresh ingredients   13
Advice on deep-frying   15

Starters   17
Stir-fry dishes   59
Curries and slow cooks   83
Soups and salads   95
Chef's specials   117
Noodle and rice dishes   131
Dips, sauces, curry pastes and extras   161
Desserts and drinks   193

Acknowledgements   205
Index   207

INTRODUCTION

From the very first bite of any of Thailand's most famous dishes, you're left in no doubt that you're in for a full-on flavour experience – bold and vibrant, with all the bases fully covered, from salty and savoury to sweet, sour and rich umami. With fragrant and aromatic ingredients including garlic, galangal, lemongrass and lime leaf, there are no bland dishes in town.

While Thai restaurants and takeaways aren't as numerous within the UK as those of other cuisines such as Indian or Chinese, that situation is thankfully changing; Thai food is becoming more widely available in high streets and towns across the country, even to the extent that some chain restaurants are becoming well known in bigger cities. As ever, it's the hungry customer who is the real winner, and of course I'd urge you to visit any and every Thai food outlet you might happen to come across, both for a delicious meal and for inspiration you can apply to your own cooking.

It's just that sort of inspiration that led me to turn my hand to some of the dishes in this book. In New Jersey, at the Topaz Thai Restaurant in Belleville, I was introduced to Mama.

Mama's enthusiasm for both food and her customers was infectious, and I quickly became obsessed with her Volcano Chicken dish – lightly crispy chicken in a slightly sweet sauce with a hint of sour tamarind. The sauce was spectacular, and with every bite of the wok-fried vegetables included in the dish, the smoke and char flavour created by the hot wok was notable. So much of a fan did I become that it proved difficult to change my order across multiple visits, until Mama insisted I switch things up and sample the Jungle Curry. In contrast to the sweetness of the Volcano Chicken, this was a powerfully spicy, thin curry and the endorphins provided by the chilli and garlic meant I left happy with my choice – even if Mama made it for me!

As well as being utterly delicious, Thai food makes such good and honest use of flavours that it's easy to become captivated and feel a personal connection to the food. Dishes that are already packed full of flavour can be customised to taste with the addition of a variety of condiments that complement the meal according to your own preferences. Fish sauce and chillies for seasoning, roasted chilli flakes for heat, lime wedges to add sharp, fresh acidity – the very act of eating and enjoying a Thai meal is a lesson in the world of flavour profiles, tastes and textures.

I hope the recipes in this book will do justice to some of the delights that Thai takeaway food has to offer and, as ever, should you decide to try any of the recipes in this book, I hope you'll be glad to have done so. I'd be delighted to hear from you if you'd like to send me pictures of your creations. You can find me online @takeawaysecret or get in touch via my website: www.kennymcgovern.com.

EQUIPMENT

Juicer – A handheld lime juicer is inexpensive and useful for everyday use in creating marinades, sauces and dressings.

Pestle and mortar – A heavy granite pestle and mortar can be used to pound ingredients, releasing oils and flavours for your soups, stir-fry dishes or curry pastes. A lighter pestle and mortar made from wood or clay can be used to lightly pound salad ingredients, as in the classic Papaya Salad (page 110).

Rice cooker – While you can cook good rice in a saucepan on the stovetop, a rice cooker is a great investment and can be used to produce perfect rice every time. Many rice cookers now come with timers and 'keep warm' functions, which are very useful when it comes to planning and preparing meals, as is the extra hob space freed up by not having to cook rice in a saucepan.

Spice grinder – Can be used to speed up the creation of curry pastes or roasted chilli flakes.

Steamer – Used for whole fish dishes, or for Sticky Rice (page 151).

Wok – A non-stick or carbon-steel wok can be used to create well-fired stir-fry dishes over a high heat. Non-stick woks can be useful and are convenient for clean-up, but a good-quality carbon-steel wok, well cared for, will last a lifetime (as described in the next section).

How to Choose, Season and Use a Carbon-Steel Wok

Non-stick woks and frying pans come in all shapes and sizes nowadays and I've certainly used a few of them over the years, with good results. If you're serious about stir-frying, however, investing in a proper carbon-steel wok is a smart decision. If you've cooked with non-stick pans often, you'll know that over time the coating inevitably wears off, making cooking difficult and risking the possibility of some of that coating going into the food you intend to eat (which is far from ideal). A properly seasoned wok creates a natural non-stick layer, which ensures you can cook over a high heat with consistent results over time.

Choosing a carbon-steel wok

Most carbon-steel woks are suitable for all hob types, but do check before buying. Woks come in various sizes, with either a round-bottom or flat-bottom finish. For home use, a flat-bottomed wok is the one to choose; round-bottomed woks are typically intended for use over the gas burners in takeaway and restaurant kitchens. When it comes to choosing the size of your wok, it's best to go for something in the small to medium range. For one-portion cooking (which is ideally how you want to stir-fry anyway), a flat-bottomed 30cm carbon-steel wok is ideal. The wok heats quickly and holds its heat so well that each portion cooks in just a few minutes, making it easy to prepare three or four portions one after another if needs be. Of course, if you have a larger hob you can choose a larger wok to suit your own needs. Expect to pay £10 to £12 for a good-quality carbon-steel wok from a Chinese super-market, or a little more online. To accompany your wok, you might choose to purchase a wok stirrer for cooking and a wok brush for cleaning.

Seasoning your carbon-steel wok

Once you've got your carbon-steel wok, you'll need to season it before you begin to cook with it. This essentially means burning off the manufacturer's coating, cleaning the wok out and heating it with oil to form a natural non-stick layer. A good seasoning on your wok will give you a pan that you can use again and again. In fact, the performance of the wok should even improve over time with extended use.

Step 1:
Give the wok a good clean in hot, soapy water, rinse and dry it completely. This is the one and only time you'll use

washing-up liquid on your wok – from this point on it should require nothing more than water, heat and a scrub with a wok brush.

With the carbon-steel wok washed and fully dried, open any nearby doors and windows and put the wok on your hob over a high heat. This is much easier to do on a gas-flame hob, but with time and patience it's possible to do it on a ceramic, electric or induction hob too. This process creates a lot of smoke and a noticeable aroma – it's unpleasant but an important part of seasoning your wok. As the wok gets hot, you'll see it begin to blacken. Tilt the pan over a high heat until all the coating is removed and the surface of the pan has changed colour; this will take a few minutes. When the coating has burnt off completely, remove the wok from the heat and set it aside to cool. Rinse the wok out with water and a wok brush, dry completely again and return it to the hob. Switch the heat on low for 5 minutes in order to help ensure the wok is completely dry before moving on to step 2 of the seasoning process . . .

Step 2:

Slice a selection of stir-fry vegetables (onions, spring onions, garlic, ginger, peppers, etc. – anything in your fridge that's looking a little less than fresh, as the ingredients won't be eaten but just used for the seasoning process. Heat the wok over a medium heat until it just begins to smoke. Add 1 tablespoon of vegetable oil and the prepared vegetables, and stir-fry for 15–20 minutes until the vegetables are almost burnt. The idea here is simply to spread the hot oil around the wok with the vegetables. Again, you'll notice the wok change colour a little and appear well used compared to the brand-new silver, shiny wok you started with. After 15–20 minutes, empty out and discard the vegetables. Allow the wok to cool, rinse out again with water and scrub with the wok brush, dry with a clean tea towel and place over a low heat for 5 minutes to dry completely. Add a little oil to the wok and wipe it all around with kitchen paper until the entire surface has a thin coating of oil. Switch the heat on to medium-low and allow the wok to sit over the heat for 10 minutes.

Your seasoned wok is now ready to use.

Using and caring for your carbon-steel wok

At this stage, with a high heat and some oil, your wok should have some good non-stick qualities. Over time, the natural patina will build on the wok and performance should improve with regular use.

Things to remember when cooking with your wok:

- Always heat the wok over a high heat until it's just smoking before adding oil. Cooking over a high heat will help to ensure that food doesn't stick.
- When adding marinated meat to the wok, allow the meat to settle in the pan for 10–15 seconds before stir-frying. Doing so will help to ensure it doesn't stick, which is particularly useful when the marinade includes corn-flour or potato starch.

- Use a wok stirrer to scrape and stir the ingredients in the wok during cooking, ensuring they don't catch in the pan any more than desired.
- After the wok is fully preheated, add enough oil for the dish you plan to cook – restaurant chefs often add more oil than is necessary to the pan then drain off any excess, ensuring the entire surface of the wok is coated.
- In the early days of owning your wok, try to avoid cooking acidic dishes (dishes with vinegar, lime juice, etc.), boiling or steaming with the wok.
- Conversely, deep-frying with lots of oil will assist in building your wok's natural non-stick patina.

To care for your wok, simply wash it out after each use with water and scrub it with a brush.

Things to remember when cleaning your wok:

- Allow the wok to cool before cleaning in order to avoid shock from drastic temperature changes, which may warp the shape of the pan.
- Use only hot water and a wok brush to clean your carbon-steel wok – washing-up liquid isn't necessary. If the wok needs more vigorous cleaning, add a little water to it and heat until boiling. This will ensure any ingredients in the wok simply slide away and it can be cleaned easily.
- Keep your wok clean and dry at all times – drying with just a tea towel isn't enough. Return the clean, dry wok

to a low heat on the hob for 5 minutes in order to ensure it's completely dry.

- Apply a little cooking oil around the entire inner surface of the wok with a piece of kitchen paper before storing the wok for future use.

By ensuring your carbon-steel wok is completely clean, dry and coated with a little oil after each use, it should remain rust-free, with a natural non-stick coating, and should last a lifetime. Should rust appear in your wok, don't panic! Simply scrub off any noticeable spots with a wire brush, wash the wok out well with a brush and hot water and allow it to dry completely. Repeat the seasoning process as outlined above and your wok will be returned to its former glory.

STORE-CUPBOARD INGREDIENTS

Chillies – Dried red chillies are used in stir-fry dishes and to make curry paste, with larger chillies offering colour and flavour while smaller ones offer a fiery chilli kick. You can also get them toasted, ground or as a condiment to serve alongside soup and noodle dishes.

Coconut milk – Rich and creamy, coconut milk can be used in curries, soups, marinades and dips. When buying coconut milk in tins or cartons, look for the percentage of coconut listed in the ingredients and try to choose a brand with a high coconut quantity and minimal added ingredients (ideally only water).

Curry paste – While you can, of course, make your own curry pastes, it's always useful to have some good-quality pastes to hand. Life gets busy, after all, and with some added ingredients a pre-made curry paste can assist in putting together a variety of dishes, from curries to dipping sauces.

Fish sauce 'nam pla' – This potent fermented fish-based seasoning adds saltiness and umami depth to soups, stir-fry sauces and more. Don't be put off by the overpowering aroma from the bottle – the added flavour imparted into dishes by good fish sauce is utterly delicious! Squid is a good brand to use.

Noodles – Rice noodles or vermicelli bean thread noodles can be used in stir-fries and soups. Bean thread vermicelli are also among the fillings used for vegetable or pork crispy spring rolls.

Oyster sauce – This thick sauce is a building block for so many stir-fry sauces, with a predominantly savoury note and just a touch of sweetness. Lee Kum Kee's Panda Brand is a good choice.

Rice (jasmine and sticky) – Steamed jasmine rice is the every-day partner to soups and stir-fry dishes, while sticky rice is delicious served with grilled meats and salad dishes, or sweetened and enriched with coconut milk for a delicious mango sticky rice dessert (page 195). Royal Umbrella and Green Dragon are good brands to use.

Soy sauce – Thin soy sauce adds salt and seasoning, thick soy sauce adds colour and a touch of sweetness, while sweet soy sauce adds a more specific sweet note.

FRESH INGREDIENTS

Basil – A large handful of fresh basil is essential in pad kra pao dishes. While holy basil is traditional (hence the name), Thai basil or Italian basil will also work, while offering different flavour notes. Holy basil and European basil have a slightly sweet aroma, while Thai basil offers a more prominent aniseed note.

Chillies – Fresh chillies are a hugely important part of Thai food. Usually called 'bird's-eye chillies' in the UK, smaller hotter chillies are used to impart heat and vibrant spice to curry pastes, stir-fries and soups, while larger, milder chillies are used to add more colour, flavour or decoration to dishes.

Coriander – Coriander roots are traditionally used in many Thai curry pastes and marinades. You can purchase these online, or as an alternative use chopped stems, which are much more widely available in the UK.

Galangal – Despite looking similar to ginger, galangal offers a citrus note along with earthy, peppery flavours. Ginger may

13

be substituted in some recipes, but the flavour profiles aren't similar so the taste will be different.

Garlic – Pungent and aromatic, used to add flavour to a variety of dishes. Thai garlic cloves are typically smaller than the garlic you'll find in UK supermarkets, so adjust recipes accordingly and to your own taste.

Lemongrass – The lower white part of the lemongrass stalk can be bruised with a knife or rolling pin, or thinly sliced. It adds a lemon-citrus flavour to marinades, soups and curry pastes.

Lime – Makrut lime zest can be added to curry pastes. Fresh lime juice is used in marinades, soups and dipping sauces, and lime wedges are an essential pad thai accompaniment.

Lime leaves – Fresh or dried makrut lime leaves offer a robust citrus flavour in soups and curry dishes.

Mint – Adds a bright, fresh finish to salad dishes.

Shallots – Sweet and only slightly sharp, shallots can contribute at all stages of the cooking process, offering flavour to marinades or a crispy finish to dishes in the form of Crispy Fried Shallots (page 174).

Spring onions – Used alongside coriander leaves to add colour and a fresh finish to a variety of dishes.

ADVICE ON DEEP-FRYING

It's not uncommon for home cooks to be a little intimidated by deep-frying. While it does pay to be cautious, with some simple tips in mind we can easily and safely deep-fry at home, even without the aid of a deep-fryer. If you plan to deep-fry often and like to keep your hob spaces free, investing in a good-quality deep-fryer is worthwhile; however, any large wok or pan can be used to good effect – simply fill the pan a third full with sunflower oil or any neutral-flavoured cooking oil that can be heated to high temperatures for deep-frying (such as vegetable oil, rapeseed oil, peanut oil or groundnut oil).

If you use a wok or a pan for deep-frying, investing in a temperature probe is a must. These can be purchased relatively inexpensively and will ensure your oil reaches the desired temperature before frying, guaranteeing crisp and golden results without any excess grease.

Most deep-frying recipes call for oil to be heated to about 180°C/350°F; however, do check individual recipe instructions for precise temperatures.

Deep-frying tips:

- Use a temperature probe to ensure your oil has reached the desired temperature before carefully adding food items.

- Avoid overcrowding the pan as this lowers the temperature of the oil and can result in greasy food. Instead, fry in batches and keep each fried batch warm in a low oven, or re-fry cooked food briefly just before serving, to reheat and crisp it up once more.

- A slotted spoon/spider strainer is useful for removing cooked food from the oil while allowing excess oil to drain off.

- A fine-mesh strainer can be used to remove smaller food remnants from the oil. This will ensure that they don't burn and keeps the oil cleaner.

- After cooking, ensure the pan with the oil is set aside in a safe place until it has completely cooled down.

- Strained oil that is free from food remnants may be reused several times; however, you'll soon find that oil that has been used to fry breaded items such as Coconut Prawns (page 58) becomes cloudy and discoloured more quickly. For this reason, I like to bulk-fry these items and often fry a double or even triple batch at one time.

STARTERS

While thinking ahead to what to choose for a main course, I'm often mesmerised by the starter selection offered on takeaway and restaurant menus, and can easily be tempted into ordering too much. This is one more reason why eating and sharing with friends is always such fun, as each additional hungry appetite gives justification to another item ordered.

When cooking at home, we have the added bonus of being able to create any number of starter dishes we choose: chicken wings, pork ribs, crispy spring rolls and, my personal favourite, chicken satay are all ready to fire your taste buds into life in preparation for other dishes to follow – provided that you've saved room!

CORN FRITTERS – TOD MAN KHAO POD

Serves 4 (makes 20 fritters)

325g tinned sweetcorn, rinsed and drained (260g drained weight)
2 teaspoons Red Curry Paste (page 179, or from a tub)
Dash of fish sauce
1 generous pinch of dried kaffir lime leaf, crushed
1 spring onion, thinly sliced
½ egg (yolk and white), whisked
1 teaspoon sea salt
4 tablespoons plain flour
4 tablespoons potato flour or cornflour
½ teaspoon baking powder
Vegetable oil for deep-frying

- Put half of the rinsed and drained sweetcorn in a blender, along with the curry paste, fish sauce, kaffir lime leaf, spring onion, egg and sea salt. Blend until combined then pour the mix into a large bowl.

- Add the remaining sweetcorn, plain flour, potato flour or cornflour, and baking powder. Combine well and check the consistency of the mixture, adding a touch more flour if necessary – the batter should fall off a spoon in one lump. Cover and set aside in the fridge for 10 minutes (the mix will keep well in the fridge overnight if you want to prepare ahead).

- Heat the oil for deep-frying to 160°C/320°F. Working in batches, carefully drop a heaped teaspoon of the prepared mix into the hot oil. Fry for 3–4 minutes, turning occasionally until golden and crispy on all sides. Don't overcrowd the pan, fry just a few fritters at a time and keep them warm in the oven on a low heat if necessary while you finish frying the remaining fritters.

- Arrange the corn fritters on a serving plate and serve with Sweet Chilli Sauce (page 169) on the side.

VEGETABLE SPRING ROLLS – POH PIA TOD

Serves 3–4 (makes 12 spring rolls)

Small handful dried black fungus strips
1 x 50g nest vermicelli bean threads
1 tablespoon oyster sauce
1 tablespoon thin soy sauce
1 tablespoon fish sauce
Pinch of white pepper
Pinch of black pepper
1 teaspoon water
1 tablespoon vegetable oil
2 shallots or 1 onion, thinly sliced
2 garlic cloves, finely chopped
75g button mushrooms, chopped
1 medium carrot, cut into thin matchsticks or grated
Small handful tinned bamboo shoots, rinsed and drained
    (50g drained weight)
12 x 21.5cm frozen spring roll wrappers, defrosted
1 tablespoon rice flour mixed with 3 tablespoons water
Vegetable oil for deep-frying

- Put the dried black fungus strips in a bowl. Cover with boiling water and set aside until completely cool.

- Put the vermicelli bean threads in a separate bowl. Cover with boiling water and soak for 5 minutes, stirring once or twice until the noodles are softened. Drain, rinse briefly with cold water, drain once more, cut the noodles and fungus two or three times into smaller pieces and set aside.

- Put the oyster sauce, thin soy sauce, fish sauce, white pepper, black pepper and water in a separate small bowl. Mix well and set aside.

- Heat a wok or large frying pan over a medium-high heat. Add the oil and sliced shallots or onion, garlic, mushrooms, carrot and bamboo shoots and stir-fry for 20–30 seconds. Add the soaked noodles and black fungus, and mix well. Add the prepared sauce, mix well once more and stir-fry for 2 minutes until the sauce is reduced and the ingredients are sizzling hot.

- Set the mix aside to cool completely. Place the defrosted spring roll wrappers on a work surface and keep covered with a clean, slightly damp cloth while you work.

- Arrange a spring roll wrapper on the work surface with one corner of the wrapper closest to you. Brush the top of the wrapper with the flour and water mix and place a generous tablespoon of the prepared filling in the lower third of the wrapper. Fold up from the bottom over the filling, then fold in the sides and continue rolling to form the spring roll, pressing down gently to seal with more of the flour and water mixture. Cover with a clean, damp tea towel and repeat the process with the remaining spring roll wrappers and mixture. At this stage the spring rolls can be frozen if desired. Freeze them on a baking tray and then place into food bags once fully frozen. The spring rolls can be fried from frozen as desired.

To fry the spring rolls:

- Heat the oil for deep-frying to 180°C/350°F. Carefully drop the spring rolls into the hot oil and fry for 2–3 minutes (from fresh) or 3–4 minutes (from frozen), turning occasionally until golden and crispy on all sides. Remove from the oil with a slotted spoon, drain off any excess oil and arrange the spring rolls on a serving plate. Serve with Sweet Chilli Sauce (page 169).

FRESH SPRING ROLLS – POH PIA SOD

These delicate rice paper wrapped spring rolls are perfect in summertime when the weather is good.

Serves 1–2 (makes 7 spring rolls)

1 x 50g nest vermicelli bean threads
1 small carrot, cut into matchsticks or grated
1 baby cucumber, thinly sliced (or ¼ cucumber, deseeded and thinly sliced)
Small handful fresh lettuce leaves, roughly chopped
Small handful fresh basil leaves, roughly chopped (see note on page 13)
Small handful fresh mint leaves, roughly chopped
1 spring onion, thinly sliced
Small handful fresh coriander leaves, roughly chopped
7 x 16cm rice paper rounds

- Put the vermicelli bean threads in a bowl. Cover with boiling water and soak for 5 minutes, stirring once or twice until the noodles are softened. Drain, rinse briefly with cold water, drain once more, then cut the noodles two or three times into smaller pieces and set aside.

- Put the carrot, cucumber, fresh lettuce, basil, mint, spring onion and coriander in a large bowl. Mix briefly.

- Fill another large bowl with warm water. Working one at a time, dip the rice paper rounds into the warm water and hold there for 5–6 seconds. Remove from the water, allow excess water to drip off and arrange the rice paper round on a work surface. Lift a small handful of the mix on to the bottom third of the wrapper. Fold up from the bottom over the filling, then fold in the sides and continue rolling to form the spring roll. Set aside and repeat the process until all of the spring rolls are prepared.

- Transfer the spring rolls to a serving plate and serve with Peanut Dipping Sauce (page 162) or Seafood Dipping Sauce (page 167).

FRIED TOFU – TAO HOO TOD

These fried tofu pieces have a crispy texture on the outside and are delicious served with dipping sauce, or they can be added to your favourite stir-fry dishes.

Serves 1–2

150g extra firm tofu
1 tablespoon rice flour
1 tablespoon cornflour or potato starch
Vegetable oil for deep-frying

- Drain the tofu, removing any liquid from the packaging, and pat dry with kitchen paper. Cut into rectangles and pat dry once more. Transfer the tofu pieces to a bowl, add the rice flour and cornflour or potato starch and mix well.

- Heat the oil for deep-frying to 180°C/350°F. Carefully drop the tofu pieces into the hot oil and fry for 5–6 minutes, or until crispy and golden on all sides. Remove from the oil with a slotted spoon, drain off any excess oil and arrange on a cutting board. Cut the crispy tofu pieces diagonally, transfer to a serving plate and serve with Sweet Chilli Sauce (page 169) or Peanut Dipping Sauce (page 162).

MUSHROOM CURRY PUFFS – KARIPAP

Serves 1–2 (makes 7 curry puffs)

1 small potato, peeled and diced
1 small carrot, peeled and diced
1 teaspoon vegetable oil
1 shallot, finely chopped
1 garlic clove, finely chopped
1 teaspoon fresh coriander stems, thinly sliced
4 button mushrooms, chopped
1 generous teaspoon curry powder
Pinch of turmeric
Pinch of sea salt
½ teaspoon caster sugar
1 teaspoon thin soy sauce
Dash of fish sauce
1 tablespoon water
375g ready-rolled puff pastry
1 egg

- Put the potato and carrot in a saucepan. Cover with water, bring to the boil, reduce the heat to medium and simmer for 10–12 minutes, or until the potato and carrot are soft. Drain and return to the pan. Mash with a potato masher and set aside.

- Heat a wok or large frying pan over a medium heat. Add the vegetable oil, shallot, garlic and coriander stems. Stir-fry for 20–30 seconds until aromatic. Add the mushrooms and stir-fry for 2 minutes. Add the curry powder, turmeric, sea salt, caster sugar, thin soy sauce, fish sauce and water. Stir-fry for a further 1–2 minutes, or until the liquid is almost completely absorbed. Remove from the heat, add the mashed potato and carrot, mix well and set aside to cool completely.

- Roll out the puff pastry dough ¼-inch (0.6cm) thick and use a pastry cutter to cut seven separate 5-inch (13cm) rounds. Fill each pastry round with a generous tablespoon of the prepared filling, fold the pastry over the filling and crimp with a fork to seal the edges.

- Heat the oven to 200°C/400°F. Crack the egg into a small bowl and whisk for a few seconds. Brush each curry puff with a little beaten egg, transfer to the oven and bake for around 20 minutes, or until puffed up and golden.

- Transfer the curry puffs to a serving plate and serve with Sweet Chilli Sauce (page 169).

MONEY BAGS – TUNG TONG

Serves 1–2

2 shallots, finely chopped
1 garlic clove, finely chopped
1 teaspoon fresh coriander stems, thinly sliced
2 teaspoons vegetable oil
60g pork mince
1 button mushroom, chopped
½ teaspoon oyster sauce
½ teaspoon thin soy sauce
Dash of fish sauce
Pinch of white pepper
Pinch of caster sugar
2–3 spring onions
7 frozen wonton skins, defrosted
Oil for deep-frying

- Put the shallots, garlic and fresh coriander stems in a pestle and mortar. Pound to a fine paste. Transfer the paste to a small bowl and set aside.

- Heat a wok or large frying pan over a medium heat. Add the oil and the prepared paste and stir-fry for 20–30 seconds until aromatic. Add the pork mince and chopped mushroom and stir-fry for 1 minute. Add the oyster sauce, thin soy sauce, fish sauce, white pepper and caster sugar and stir-fry for 1–2 minutes, or until the pork is cooked and the sauce has been absorbed. Set aside to cool completely.

- Slice the long green part of each spring onion into two or three strips. Put the spring onion strips in a bowl and cover with boiling water. Let stand for a few seconds to soften, then drain, rinse briefly with cold water, drain once more and set aside.

- Arrange a wonton skin on a work surface. Scoop two teaspoons of the prepared mix into the centre of the wonton skin, pull the wrapper up around the filling, twist and pinch to seal and tie with a strip of spring onion. Repeat the process until all of the 'money bags' are prepared.

- Heat the oil for deep-frying to 170°C/340°F. Carefully drop the money bags into the hot oil and fry for 5–6 minutes, or until golden and crispy on all sides. Remove from the oil with a slotted spoon, drain off any excess oil and arrange on a serving plate. Serve with Sweet Chilli Sauce (page 169).

PORK AND VEGETABLE CRISPY
SPRING ROLLS – POH PIA TOD

Serves 3–4 (makes 12 spring rolls)

Small handful dried black fungus strips
1 x 50g nest vermicelli bean threads
1 tablespoon oyster sauce
1 tablespoon thin soy sauce
1 tablespoon fish sauce
Pinch of white pepper
Pinch of black pepper
1 teaspoon water
1 tablespoon vegetable oil
125g pork mince
2 shallots or 1 onion, thinly sliced
2 garlic cloves, finely chopped
1 small carrot, cut into thin matchsticks or grated
Small handful tinned bamboo shoots, rinsed and drained
    (50g drained weight)
12 x 21.5cm frozen spring roll wrappers, defrosted
1 tablespoon rice flour mixed with 3 tablespoons water
Oil for deep-frying

- Put the dried black fungus strips in a bowl. Cover with boiling water and set aside until completely cool. Once cool, drain, rinse briefly with cold water, drain once more and set aside.

- Put the vermicelli bean threads in another bowl. Cover with boiling water and soak for 5 minutes, stirring once or twice until the noodles are softened. Drain, rinse briefly with cold water, drain once more, cut the noodles two or three times into smaller pieces and set aside.

- Put the oyster sauce, thin soy sauce, fish sauce, white pepper, black pepper and water in a separate small bowl. Mix well and set aside.

- Heat a wok or large frying pan over a medium-high heat. Add the oil and pork mince and stir-fry for 1–2 minutes until browned. Add the sliced shallot or onion, garlic, carrot and bamboo shoots and stir-fry for 20–30 seconds. Add the soaked noodles and black fungus and mix well. Add the prepared sauce, mix well once more and stir-fry for 2 minutes until the sauce is reduced and the ingredients are sizzling hot.

- Set the mix aside to cool completely. Place the defrosted spring roll wrappers on a work surface and keep covered with a clean, slightly damp cloth while you work.

- Arrange a spring roll wrapper on the work surface with one corner of the wrapper closest to you. Brush the top of the wrapper with the flour and water mix and place a generous tablespoon of the prepared filling in the lower third of the wrapper. Fold up from the bottom over the filling, then fold in the sides and continue rolling to form the spring roll, pressing down gently to seal with more of the flour and water mixture. Cover with a clean, damp tea towel and repeat the process with the remaining spring roll wrappers and mixture. At this stage the spring rolls can be frozen if desired. Freeze on a baking tray and then place into food bags once fully frozen. The spring rolls can be fried from frozen as desired.

To fry the spring rolls:

- Heat the oil for deep-frying to 180°C/350°F. Carefully drop the spring rolls into the hot oil and fry for 2–3 minutes (from fresh) or 3–4 minutes (from frozen), turning occasionally until golden and crispy on all sides. Remove from the oil with a slotted spoon, drain off any excess oil and arrange the spring rolls on a serving plate. Serve with Sweet Chilli Sauce (page 169).

CRISPY PORK BELLY – MOO GROB

Serves 1–2 (makes 10 pieces)

250g pork belly slices
Oil for deep-frying
Pinch of sea salt

- Cut each pork belly slice into five equal pieces. Arrange the pieces on a plate, fat side up, and place uncovered in the fridge overnight. Remove the pork from the fridge 20 minutes before cooking.

- *To air fry:* Brush the fatty top section of each pork belly piece with a little vegetable oil and season with a touch of salt. Arrange the pork belly pieces fat side up in an air fryer tray. Air fry for 10 minutes at 180°C/350°F. Increase the heat to 200°C/400°F and air fry for a further 5–6 minutes, checking the pork every minute or so until it's as crispy as you like it.

- *To deep-fry:* Heat the oil for deep-frying to 150°C/300°F. Carefully transfer the pork belly pieces to the hot oil and fry for 7–8 minutes. Increase the temperature of the oil to 180°C/350°F and keep cooking for another 2–3 minutes, or until the pork is as crispy as you like it.

- Transfer the crispy pork to a serving plate. Serve with Spicy Dipping Sauce (page 165) and Sticky Rice (see pages 150 and 151).

SALT AND CHILLI PORK RIBS
– KRONG MOO TOD

One of the UK's growing number of Thai street-food chains recently added this dish to its menu and I knew after one bite that it would be next on my list of things to try to recreate.

Serves 1–2

For the seasoning
    1 teaspoon sea salt
    ½ teaspoon caster sugar
    ½ teaspoon MSG
    ¼ teaspoon cumin powder
    ¼ teaspoon coriander powder
    ¼ teaspoon garlic powder
    ¼ teaspoon galangal powder
    ½ teaspoon roasted chilli powder
    Pinch of white pepper

To cook
    700g pork spare ribs
    1 lemongrass stalk, bruised (white part only)
    2 makrut lime leaves
    ½ teaspoon sea salt
    ½ teaspoon caster sugar
    1 litre water
    Oil for deep-frying

1 tablespoon vegetable oil
1 shallot, finely chopped
2 garlic cloves, finely chopped
Small handful fresh coriander leaves, roughly chopped

- To make the seasoning, put the sea salt, sugar, MSG, cumin powder, coriander powder, garlic powder, galangal powder, roasted chilli powder and white pepper in a bowl. Mix well and set aside.

- Put the pork ribs in a large saucepan, cover completely with water and set aside for 20 minutes. Drain the water and return the pork ribs to the pan.

- Add the lemongrass, lime leaves, sea salt, caster sugar and water. Mix well. Bring to the boil, reduce the heat to low and cover almost completely with a lid.

- Simmer the pork ribs for 1 hour 50 minutes, or until the pork meat is tender but not quite falling off the bone. Using tongs, remove the cooked spare ribs from the liquid and set aside on a plate to cool.

- Heat the oil for deep-frying to 160°C/320°F. Carefully add the ribs to the hot oil in batches and fry for about 5 minutes until the ribs are piping hot and just beginning to crisp up around the edges, turning the ribs occasionally. Increase the oil temperature to 180°C/350°F and fry the ribs for a further 2 minutes until nicely coloured and slightly crisp. Repeat until all of the ribs are fried.

35

- Remove the ribs from the oil using tongs and set aside.

- Heat a wok or large frying pan over a medium heat. Add 1 tablespoon vegetable oil, the shallot and garlic. Stir-fry for 20–30 seconds until aromatic. Add the cooked pork ribs. Season with 1 teaspoon of the prepared seasoning (or to taste) and stir-fry for a further 20–30 seconds.

- Transfer the ribs to a serving plate, garnish with the fresh coriander leaves and serve.

PORK SKEWERS – MOO PING

Serves 1–2

For the marinade
　　2 garlic cloves, peeled
　　1 teaspoon fresh coriander stems, thinly sliced
　　2 teaspoons oyster sauce
　　1 teaspoon thin soy sauce
　　1 teaspoon thick soy sauce
　　½ teaspoon palm sugar or light brown sugar
　　Pinch of white pepper

To cook
　　225g pork tenderloin fillet
　　½ teaspoon potato flour or cornflour
　　2 tablespoons coconut milk

- Put the garlic and fresh coriander stems in a pestle and mortar. Pound to a fine paste. Transfer to a wide bowl and add the oyster sauce, thin soy sauce, thick soy sauce, sugar and white pepper.

- Trim any excess fat from the pork loin and cut into thin strips. Add to the marinade ingredients and mix thoroughly. Cover and set aside for 1 hour, or overnight. Remove the marinated pork from the fridge 20 minutes before you want to cook.

- Soak six small wooden skewers in water 30 minutes before you want to start cooking, to ensure they don't burn.

- Add the potato flour or cornflour and coconut milk to the marinated pork. Mix well to combine and ribbon each pork strip on to the pre-soaked skewers, ensuring each piece is pierced several times by the skewer (each skewer should comfortably hold two or three pork strips). Repeat the process until all of the meat is arranged on the skewers.

- *To air fry:* Arrange the pork skewers in the air fryer drawer. Air fry at 190°C/375°F for 10–12 minutes, turning once or twice until the pork is cooked through and nicely coloured on all sides.

- *To pan fry:* Heat a griddle pan or large frying pan over a medium heat. Add the pork skewers and fry for 8–10 minutes, turning occasionally until the pork is cooked through and nicely coloured on all sides.

- *To cook on an outdoor grill:* Cook the pork skewers on the grill over a medium heat for 8–10 minutes, turning occasionally until the pork is cooked through and nicely coloured on all sides.

- Arrange the pork skewers on a serving plate and serve with Spicy Dipping Sauce (page 165).

DRIED FRIED PORK – MOO DAD DEAW

Traditionally dried in the hot sun, these pork slices have a jerky-like texture. After they have dried out slowly in the oven, it takes just a few seconds to flash-fry and crisp them up, ready to serve to hungry guests.

Serves 1–2

1 garlic clove, crushed
1 teaspoon oyster sauce
1 teaspoon thin soy sauce
Dash of thick soy sauce
Dash of fish sauce
½ teaspoon palm sugar
¼ teaspoon white pepper
1 tablespoon water
250g pork tenderloin fillet, thinly sliced
Oil for deep-frying
1 spring onion, thinly sliced
1 teaspoon toasted sesame seeds

- Put the crushed garlic, oyster sauce, thin soy sauce, thick soy sauce, fish sauce, sugar, white pepper and water in a bowl. Mix well. Add the sliced pork and mix thoroughly once more. Cover and set aside in the fridge for at least 1 hour, or overnight. Remove the pork from the fridge 20 minutes before you want to cook.

- Put the oven on a low heat, around 80°C/175°F. Brush a grill tray with a touch of oil and arrange the pork slices evenly on the rack. Place in the oven and cook for 1 hour.

- Heat the oil for deep-frying to 160°C/320°F. Carefully drop the dried pork pieces into the hot oil in batches and fry for 1–2 minutes, or until the pork is nicely coloured and crispy. Remove from the oil with a slotted spoon and set aside on a plate. Repeat the process until all the pork pieces are fried.

- Arrange the fried pork pieces on a bed of lettuce leaves or on a serving plate, garnish with the spring onion and toasted sesame seeds, and serve with Sweet Chilli Sauce (page 169).

NORTHERN THAI-STYLE SAUSAGE MEATBALLS

This twist on sai ua (Thai grilled sausage) is aromatic and spicy.

Serves 1–2 (makes 9 small meatballs)

1 small shallot, finely chopped
1 garlic clove, finely chopped
1 fresh makrut lime leaf, thinly sliced and chopped
1 teaspoon fresh coriander stems, finely chopped
1 generous teaspoon Red Curry Paste (page 179, or from a tub)
1 teaspoon fish sauce
Pinch of turmeric
Pinch of white pepper
Pinch of black pepper
125g pork mince (20% fat)
25g cooked sticky rice (see pages 150 and 151)
1 teaspoon vegetable oil

- Put the shallot, garlic, lime leaf and coriander stems in a pestle and mortar. Pound to a rough paste.

- Transfer this paste to a large bowl. Add the red curry paste, fish sauce, turmeric, white pepper and black pepper. Mix well. Add the pork mince and cooked sticky rice and mix thoroughly until well combined. Cover and set aside in the fridge for 1 hour, or overnight.

- Form nine small meatballs with the prepared mix.

- Heat the vegetable oil in a frying pan over a medium-low heat. Carefully drop the prepared meatballs into the frying pan and fry for 8–10 minutes, turning occasionally until the sausage pieces are sizzling, slightly crisp and cooked through.

- Transfer the sausage meatballs to a serving plate and serve with Sweet Chilli Sauce (page 169).

CHICKEN CRISPY SPRING ROLLS – POH PIA TOD

Serves 3–4 (makes 12 spring rolls)

Small handful dried black fungus strips
1 x 50g nest vermicelli bean threads
1 tablespoon oyster sauce
1 tablespoon thin soy sauce
1 tablespoon fish sauce
Pinch of white pepper
Pinch of black pepper
1 teaspoon water
1 tablespoon vegetable oil
1 large skinless, boneless chicken thigh, thinly sliced
2 shallots or 1 onion, thinly sliced
2 garlic cloves, finely chopped
1 small carrot, cut into thin matchsticks or grated
Small handful tinned bamboo shoots, rinsed and drained
    (about 50g drained weight)
12 x 21.5cm frozen spring roll wrappers, defrosted
1 tablespoon rice flour mixed with 3 tablespoons water
Oil for deep-frying

- Put the dried black fungus strips in a bowl. Cover with boiling water and set aside for 20–30 minutes. Rinse with cold water, drain and set aside.

- Put the vermicelli bean threads in a bowl. Cover with boiling water and soak for 5 minutes, stirring once or twice until the noodles are softened. Drain, rinse briefly with cold water, drain once more, cut the noodles two or three times into smaller pieces and set aside.

- Put the oyster sauce, thin soy sauce, fish sauce, white pepper, black pepper and water in a separate small bowl. Mix well and set aside.

- Heat a wok or large frying pan over a medium-high heat. Add the vegetable oil and sliced chicken and stir-fry for 1–2 minutes until browned. Add the sliced shallots or onion, garlic, carrot and bamboo shoots. Stir-fry for 20–30 seconds. Add the soaked noodles and black fungus and mix well. Add the prepared sauce, mix well once more and stir-fry for 2 minutes until the sauce is absorbed and the ingredients are sizzling hot.

- Set the mix aside to cool completely. Place the defrosted spring roll wrappers on a work surface and keep covered with a clean, slightly damp cloth while you work.

- Arrange a spring roll wrapper on the work surface with one corner of the wrapper closest to you. Brush the top of the wrapper with the flour and water mix and place a generous tablespoon of the prepared filling in the lower third of the wrapper. Fold up from the bottom over the filling, then fold in the sides and continue rolling to form the spring roll, pressing down gently to seal with more of the flour and water mixture. Cover with a clean, damp tea towel and repeat the process with the remaining spring roll wrappers and mixture. At this stage the spring rolls can be frozen if desired. Freeze on a baking tray and then place into food bags once fully frozen. The spring rolls can be fried from frozen as desired.

To fry the spring rolls:

- Heat the oil for deep-frying to 180°C/350°F. Carefully drop the spring rolls into the hot oil and fry for 2–3 minutes (from fresh) or 3–4 minutes (from frozen), turning occasionally until golden and crispy on all sides. Remove from the oil with a slotted spoon, drain off any excess oil and arrange the spring rolls on a serving plate. Serve with Sweet Chilli Sauce (page 169).

CRISPY CHICKEN WINGS – GAI TOD

Serves 4 (makes about 24 wings in total, depending on size)

1kg chicken wings, wing tips removed
1 tablespoon Red Curry Paste (page 179, or from a tub)
1 teaspoon oyster sauce
1 teaspoon thin soy sauce
Dash of fish sauce
1 tablespoon water
Oil for deep-frying
2 makrut lime leaves, thinly sliced
250g plain flour
Small handful fresh coriander leaves, roughly chopped

- Joint the chicken wings using a sharp knife to separate the drumettes and wingettes. Put all the wing pieces in a large bowl and add the red curry paste, oyster sauce, thin soy sauce, fish sauce and water. Mix well and set aside in the fridge for 1 hour, or overnight. Remove the chicken wings from the fridge 20 minutes before you want to cook.

- Heat the oil for deep-frying to 160°C/320°F. Carefully drop the sliced makrut lime leaves into the oil and fry for just a second or two until crispy. Use a fine sieve to remove the crispy lime leaves from the oil and set aside.

- Increase the heat to 180°C/350°F. Working in batches, press some of the chicken wings into the flour, mixing well and pressing down hard until the wings are fully coated. Carefully drop the coated chicken wings into the hot oil and fry for about 10 minutes, or until just cooked through and golden. Use tongs or a slotted spoon to remove the chicken wings from the oil, draining off any excess oil, and set them aside on a plate. Keep warm in a low oven while you repeat the process until all of the wings are fried.

- Arrange the red curry chicken wings on a serving plate, garnish with crispy lime leaves and fresh coriander and serve.

- Leftover wings will reheat well in a hot oven or air fryer (about 180°C/350°F for 10–12 minutes).

CHICKEN SATAY – SATAY GAI

One of my favourite dishes and one I'll order from the menu every time. Thai chicken satay is often served with some grilled bread slices, which are a delicious way to mop up leftover peanut sauce.

Serves 1–2

225g skinless, boneless chicken thigh fillets
1 teaspoon curry powder
¼ teaspoon turmeric
¼ teaspoon galangal powder (optional)
Pinch of sea salt
Pinch of white pepper
¼ teaspoon caster sugar
2 tablespoons coconut milk
1 tablespoon vegetable oil
1 tablespoon water

- Cut each of the chicken thighs into four or five thin strips. Add the curry powder, turmeric, galangal powder (if using), sea salt, white pepper, caster sugar, coconut milk, vegetable oil and water and mix well. Cover and set aside in the fridge for 1 hour, or overnight. Remove the marinated chicken from the fridge 20 minutes before you want to cook.

- Soak small bamboo skewers in cold water for 20 minutes (this will keep them from burning during cooking). Ribbon the marinated chicken pieces on to the bamboo skewers.

- *To air fry:* Arrange the chicken skewers in the air fryer drawer. Air fry at 180°C/350°F for 10–12 minutes, turning once or twice until the chicken is cooked through and nicely coloured on all sides.

- *To pan fry:* Heat a griddle pan or frying pan over a medium heat. Add the chicken skewers and fry for 10–12 minutes, turning occasionally until the chicken is cooked through and nicely coloured on all sides.

- *To cook on an outdoor grill:* Cook the skewers on the grill over a medium heat for 8–10 minutes, turning occasionally until the chicken is cooked through and nicely coloured on all sides.

- Arrange the cooked chicken satay skewers on a serving plate and serve with toasted bread, Peanut Dipping Sauce (page 162) and Cucumber Relish (page 170).

GRILLED CHICKEN – GAI YANG

Serves 2–3

1 shallot, finely chopped
2 garlic cloves, finely chopped
1 teaspoon fresh coriander stems, finely chopped
1 lemongrass stalk (white part only), finely chopped
2 teaspoons thin soy sauce
½ teaspoon thick soy sauce
2 teaspoons fish sauce
Pinch of coriander powder
Pinch of turmeric
1 teaspoon palm sugar or brown sugar
Pinch of white pepper
Pinch of black pepper
450g skinless, boneless chicken thigh fillets
1 teaspoon vegetable oil

- Put the shallot, garlic, coriander stems and lemongrass in a pestle and mortar. Pound to a rough paste. Transfer to a large bowl and add the thin soy sauce, thick soy sauce, fish sauce, coriander powder, turmeric, sugar, white pepper and black pepper. Mix well.

- Add the chicken thighs to the bowl and mix well until evenly coated. Cover and set aside in the fridge for 2 hours, or ideally overnight. Remove from the fridge 20 minutes before you want to cook, add the vegetable oil and mix well.

- *To air fry:* Arrange the chicken thighs in the air fryer drawer. Air fry at 200°C/400°F for 12–14 minutes, turning once or twice until the chicken is cooked through and nicely coloured on all sides.

- *To pan fry:* Heat a griddle pan or frying pan over a medium heat. Add the chicken thighs and fry for 12–14 minutes, turning occasionally until the chicken is cooked through and nicely coloured on all sides.

- *To cook on an outdoor grill:* Cook the skewers on the grill over a medium heat for 10–12 minutes, turning occasionally until the chicken is cooked through and nicely coloured on all sides.

To serve:

- Arrange the cooked chicken on a serving plate and serve with Spicy Dipping Sauce (page 165).

SWEET CHILLI CHICKEN BALLS
– LUK CHIN GAI TOD

Serves 1–2 (makes 7 meatballs)

1 large skinless, boneless chicken breast fillet (around
   150g)
1 spring onion, thinly sliced
Pinch of cumin power
Pinch of coriander powder
Dash of thin soy sauce
1½ teaspoons sweet chilli sauce
½ teaspoon fresh lime juice
1 heaped tablespoon panko breadcrumbs
Small handful fresh coriander leaves, finely chopped
Vegetable oil for deep-frying

- Cut the chicken into small pieces and place into a food
  processor with the spring onion, cumin powder, coriander
  powder, thin soy sauce, sweet chilli sauce, lime juice, panko
  breadcrumbs and almost all of the fresh coriander. Pulse
  seven or eight times until the chicken is minced and mixed
  with the other ingredients. Oil your hands slightly and form
  meatballs about the size of a golf ball.

- Heat the oil for deep-frying to 180°C/350°F. Carefully
  place the chicken balls into the hot oil and fry for 3–4
  minutes, or until cooked through and golden.

- Drain off any excess oil and arrange the fried chicken balls on a serving plate. Garnish with a little more fresh coriander and serve with Sweet Chilli Sauce (page 169).

CHICKEN AND PRAWN TOASTS –
KANOM PUNG NAH GOONG GAI

These cute little toasts are great to make ahead and store in the freezer for future use as they fry from frozen in just a few minutes.

Makes about 16 pieces

2 garlic cloves, finely chopped
2 makrut lime leaves, thinly sliced
250g minced chicken
80g fresh (not frozen) raw king prawns
1 teaspoon oyster sauce
Dash of fish sauce
½ teaspoon sea salt
¼ teaspoon white pepper
¼ teaspoon black pepper
¼ teaspoon caster sugar
1 teaspoon rice flour
1 tablespoon water
16 'toastie loaf' small white bread slices
250g sesame seeds
Oil for deep-frying

- Put the garlic, lime leaves, minced chicken, king prawns, oyster sauce, fish sauce, sea salt, white pepper, black pepper, caster sugar, rice flour and water in a blender and blend to a smooth paste.

- Using a flat spatula, spread about two teaspoons of the prepared prawn mix on to a bread slice, spreading it all the way to the edges of the bread. Pour the sesame seeds on to a large plate and press the bread, topped side down, firmly into the sesame seeds to coat. Flip the prepared toast slice over, cut into four triangles and arrange on a tray lined with baking paper.

- Continue preparing the toasts – once you run out of space on the baking tray, you can add another sheet of baking paper on the prepared toasts and build the next layer on top, until you have used up all of the mix and bread. Cover the top layer with a final sheet of baking paper.

- Place the whole tray of prepared toasts into the freezer and freeze for 6 hours, or overnight. After that, you can remove the baking tray and paper and transfer all the prepared toasts into one freezer-safe food bag for easy storage.

- To cook the chicken and prawn toasts from frozen, heat the oil for deep-frying to 165°C/330°F. Carefully place some of the frozen toasts into the hot oil with the chicken and pork mix facing down and fry for 2½ minutes. Carefully flip the toasts over with tongs and fry for another 2 minutes, or until they are golden and crispy. Remove the toasts from the oil with tongs and arrange on a plate lined with kitchen paper. Repeat until all of your toasts are fried. Serve with Sweet Chilli Sauce (page 169).

FISH CAKES – TOD MUN PLA

Serves 3–4 (makes 12 fish cakes)

250g white fish fillet (cod, haddock, lemon sole and
   pollock work well)
1 tablespoon Red Curry Paste (page 179, or from a tub)
1 teaspoon fish sauce
½ teaspoon thin soy sauce
¼ teaspoon sugar
1 generous tablespoon rice flour
4 green beans, thinly sliced (about 25g)
2 makrut lime leaves, thinly sliced
½ egg (see tip)
Vegetable oil for deep-frying

- Cut the fish into small pieces and place in a pestle and
  mortar. Pound to a fine paste, add the red curry paste, fish
  sauce, thin soy sauce, sugar and rice flour and pound again
  until well mixed.

- Pour the paste into a large bowl. Add the green beans,
  makrut lime leaves and egg and mix thoroughly once more.
  Sir the mix well with a fork until the paste is sticky and
  smooth.

- Heat the oil for deep-frying to 180°C/350°F. Working in batches, carefully drop tablespoons of the fish cake mix into the hot oil and fry for 2–3 minutes, or until cooked through and golden.

- Remove from the oil with a slotted spoon. Drain off any excess oil and keep warm in a low oven. Repeat the process with the remaining mix until all the fish cakes are fried.

- Arrange the fish cakes on a serving plate and serve with Cucumber Relish (page 170) and Sweet Chilli Sauce (page 169).

- **Tip:** I typically save any leftover egg to use in fried rice dishes or for a small, simple omelette to accompany jasmine rice.

COCONUT PRAWNS

Crispy coated prawns with a delicate coconut flavour.

Serves 1–2 (makes 9 coconut prawns)

60g rice flour
60g panko breadcrumbs
40g desiccated coconut
1 egg
160g raw king prawns, deveined
Oil for deep-frying

- Spread the rice flour out on a plate. Put the panko bread-crumbs and desiccated coconut in a bowl and mix well. In a separate bowl, whisk the egg.

- Keeping one hand dry, dip each king prawn first into the rice flour then into the egg, and finally into the breadcrumb and coconut mix. Press down firmly to coat each prawn with the mix and set aside on a plate.

- Heat the oil for deep-frying to 180°C/350°F. Carefully drop the breaded prawns into the hot oil and fry for 2–3 minutes, turning occasionally until golden brown and crispy. Remove from the oil with a slotted spoon, drain off any excess oil and arrange on a serving plate. Serve with Sweet Chilli Sauce (page 169).

STIR-FRY DISHES

The aromatic and fragrant ingredients used in Thai cooking work spectacularly well in stir-fry dishes, and offer big rewards for minimum effort. With flavour released into the oil by shallots, garlic and chillies, each dish begins life in style, made tastier still with the addition of savoury, sweet and sour sauce ingredients.

As is always the case with stir-fry cooking, having your ingredients and sauces prepared and to hand before you start is essential, as things typically move at a fast pace as soon as the oil hits the pan. With a high heat, sizzling ingredients and even a fancy wok toss to show your skills, stir-fry cooking is lots of fun, and especially useful when you want a meal on the table quickly.

Before we dive in, here's a top tip: if you're planning to eat your favourite stir-fry dishes with steamed rice, start your rice cooking before you begin doing anything else so it's fluffy and warm right when you need it.

MARINATED STIR-FRY PORK

Serves 1–2 (makes enough to follow 1 stir-fry recipe)

1 teaspoon oyster sauce
½ teaspoon thin soy sauce
Pinch of white pepper
1 teaspoon water
150g pork tenderloin fillet, thinly sliced

- Put the oyster sauce, thin soy sauce, white pepper and water in a bowl. Add the sliced pork and mix well. Cover and set aside in the fridge for 1 hour, or overnight. Remove from the fridge 20 minutes before you want to cook.

MARINATED STIR-FRY BEEF

Serve 1–2 (makes enough to follow 1 stir-fry recipe)

1 teaspoon oyster sauce
½ teaspoon thin soy sauce
Pinch of white pepper
Pinch of bicarbonate of soda
1 teaspoon vegetable oil
1 teaspoon water
1 teaspoon potato starch or cornflour
150g sirloin or rib-eye beef steak, thinly sliced

- Put the oyster sauce, thin soy sauce, white pepper, bicarbonate of soda, vegetable oil, water and potato starch or cornflour in a bowl. Add the sliced beef, mix well, cover and set aside in the fridge for 1 hour, or overnight. Remove from the fridge 20 minutes before you want to cook.

MARINATED STIR-FRY CHICKEN BREAST

Serves 1–2 (makes enough to follow 1 stir-fry recipe)

1 teaspoon thin soy sauce
Pinch of white pepper
1 teaspoon vegetable oil
1 teaspoon water
1 teaspoon potato starch or cornflour
125–150g skinless, boneless chicken breast fillet, thinly
  sliced

- Put the thin soy sauce, white pepper, vegetable oil, water
  and potato starch or cornflour in a bowl. Add the sliced
  chicken and mix well. Cover and set aside in the fridge for
  1 hour, or overnight. Remove from the fridge 20 minutes
  before you want to cook.

MARINATED STIR-FRY CHICKEN THIGHS

Serves 1–2 (makes enough to follow 1 stir-fry recipe)

1 teaspoon oyster sauce
½ teaspoon thin soy sauce
Pinch of white pepper
1 teaspoon water
125–150g skinless, boneless chicken thighs, thinly sliced

- Put the oyster sauce, thin soy sauce, white pepper and water in a bowl. Add the sliced chicken and mix well. Cover and set aside in the fridge for 1 hour, or overnight. Remove from the fridge 20 minutes before you want to cook.

CRISPY KING PRAWNS FOR STIR-FRY DISHES

Serves 1–2 (Makes enough for 1 stir-fry dish)

110g raw fresh king prawns
Pinch of sea salt
Pinch of white pepper
3 tablespoons potato starch
Oil for deep frying

- In a bowl, add the raw king prawns, vegetable oil, sea salt, white pepper and potato starch. Mix well until the prawns are evenly coated with the potato starch.

- Heat the oil for deep frying to 180°C/350°F. Carefully drop the king prawns into the hot oil and fry for 2–3 minutes, or until crispy and golden. Remove from the oil with a slotted spoon, drain off any excess oil and set aside until needed. Use immediately in your favourite stir-fry dishes.

CRISPY CHICKEN FOR STIR-FRY DISHES

Serves 1–2 (makes enough to follow 1 stir-fry recipe)

150g skinless, boneless chicken breast fillet, cut into bite-
    sized pieces
Pinch of sea salt
Pinch of white pepper
2 tablespoons potato starch or cornflour
Oil for deep-frying

- Put the chicken pieces, sea salt and white pepper in a bowl. Mix well. Add the potato starch or cornflour and mix well once more. Shake off any excess flour and transfer the coated chicken pieces to a separate small plate.

- Heat the oil for deep-frying to 180°C/350°F. Carefully drop the chicken pieces into the oil and fry for 2–3 minutes, or until golden and crispy. Remove from the oil with a slotted spoon, drain off any excess oil and set aside until needed. Add to your favourite stir-fry dishes.

- The crispy chicken will keep well in the fridge for up to 2 days and can be reheated briefly again in hot oil or in an air fryer.

VERMICELLI BEAN THREAD NOODLE
STIR-FRY – PAD WOON SEN

This delicious dish comes together very quickly – ideal for a quick midweek dinner or to serve alongside other dishes as a larger meal.

Serves 1–2

2 x 50g nests vermicelli bean threads
1 tablespoon oyster sauce
1 teaspoon thin soy sauce
Dash of fish sauce
1 teaspoon sweet soy sauce
¼ teaspoon sugar
Pinch of white pepper
50ml light chicken stock or water
1 tablespoon vegetable oil
2 garlic cloves, finely chopped
100g pork mince
½ small carrot, thinly sliced
Small handful cabbage leaves, roughly chopped
1 egg
1 spring onion, thinly sliced
Small handful fresh coriander leaves, roughly chopped
½ mild red chilli, sliced (optional)

- Put the vermicelli bean threads in a bowl. Cover with boiling water and soak for 5 minutes, stirring once or twice until the noodles are softened. Drain, rinse briefly with cold water, drain once more and set aside.

- Put the oyster sauce, thin soy sauce, fish sauce, sweet soy sauce, sugar, white pepper, and light chicken stock or water in a separate small bowl. Mix well and set aside.

- Heat a wok or large frying pan over a medium-high heat. Add the vegetable oil and chopped garlic. Stir-fry for 10 seconds then add the pork mince. Stir-fry for 1 minute. Add the carrot and cabbage leaves and mix well. Add the egg and stir-fry all the ingredients in the wok together for another minute.

- Add the drained bean thread noodles and stir-fry for 20–30 seconds. Add the prepared sauce and mix well. Stir-fry for 1 minute until the sauce thickens and the noodles are evenly coated.

- Pour the vermicelli bean thread stir-fry on to a serving plate, garnish with spring onion and fresh coriander, and serve with sliced red chilli if desired.

BEEF AND OYSTER SAUCE STIR-FRY – NEUA PAD NAM MUN HOI

With its mild flavour, this is perfect served alongside hotter dishes.

Serves 1–2

1 tablespoon oyster sauce
1 teaspoon thin soy sauce
1 teaspoon thick soy sauce
Dash of fish sauce
Pinch of white pepper
¼ teaspoon caster sugar
75ml light stock or water
1 tablespoon vegetable oil
150g Marinated Stir-Fry Beef (page 61)
1 small onion, roughly chopped
1 garlic clove, finely chopped
1 button mushroom, quartered
¼ red pepper, roughly chopped
¼ green pepper, roughly chopped
1 spring onion, sliced
Small handful fresh coriander leaves, roughly chopped

• Put the oyster sauce, thin soy sauce, thick soy sauce, fish sauce, white pepper, caster sugar and stock or water in a bowl. Mix well and set aside.

- Heat a wok or large frying pan over a medium-high heat. Add the vegetable oil and marinated steak. Let the sliced meat sit in the pan for 20 seconds then stir-fry for 1 minute until browned. Add the onion, garlic, mushroom and peppers and stir-fry for a further minute.

- Add the prepared sauce and mix well. Stir-fry for 1–2 minutes, until the sauce reduces slightly. Add the spring onion and mix once more.

- Pour the beef and oyster sauce stir-fry on to a serving plate, garnish with fresh coriander and serve with Jasmine Rice (pages 142 and 144).

CASHEW CHICKEN STIR-FRY –
GAI PAD MED MAMUANG

Serves 1–2

1 tablespoon oyster sauce
2 teaspoons thin soy sauce
½ teaspoon thick soy sauce
Dash of fish sauce
2 teaspoons Chilli Paste (page 163)
75ml light stock or water
1 tablespoon vegetable oil
2 large dried red chillies
1 small onion, roughly chopped
1 garlic clove, finely chopped
¼ red pepper, roughly chopped
¼ yellow pepper, roughly chopped
½ carrot, thinly sliced
1 button mushroom, quartered
Pinch of white pepper
1 portion cooked crispy chicken (page 65)
1 portion Fried Cashew Nuts (page 176)
1 spring onion, sliced

- Put the oyster sauce, thin soy sauce, thick soy sauce, fish sauce, chilli paste and light stock or water in a bowl. Mix well and set aside.

- Heat a wok or large frying pan over a medium-high heat. Add the vegetable oil, dried red chillies, onion, garlic, red pepper, yellow pepper, carrot and mushroom. Stir-fry for 1 minute.

- Add the prepared sauce and mix well. Add the white pepper and stir-fry for another 1–2 minutes until the sauce is slightly reduced. Add the cooked crispy chicken pieces and mix well. Add the cashew nuts and mix once more.

- Pour the cashew chicken stir-fry on to a serving plate, garnish with spring onion and serve with Jasmine Rice (pages 142 and 144).

SWEET AND SOUR CHICKEN STIR-FRY – GAI PAD PREOW WAN

Serves 1–2

1 tablespoon oyster sauce
1 teaspoon thin soy sauce
½ teaspoon thick soy sauce
½ teaspoon sweet soy sauce
Dash of fish sauce
½ teaspoon sriracha sauce
½ teaspoon sweet chilli sauce
½ teaspoon white vinegar
¼ teaspoon caster sugar
75ml light stock or water
1 tablespoon vegetable oil
125–150g Marinated Stir-Fry Chicken Thighs (page 63)
1 onion, finely chopped
1 garlic clove, finely chopped
¼ red pepper, finely chopped
¼ green pepper, finely chopped
Small handful pineapple chunks, fresh or from a tin
Small handful dry roasted or fried cashew nuts (page 176)

- Put the oyster sauce, thin soy sauce, thick soy sauce, sweet soy sauce, fish sauce, sriracha sauce, sweet chilli sauce, white vinegar, caster sugar and light stock or water in a bowl. Mix well and set aside.

- Heat a wok or large frying pan over a medium heat. Add the vegetable oil and marinated chicken thighs. Let the chicken sit in the pan for 20 seconds then stir-fry for 2 minutes until browned. Add the onion, garlic, red pepper and green pepper. Stir-fry for 1 minute.

- Add the prepared sauce and mix well. Stir-fry for 1–2 minutes, or until the sauce reduces slightly. Add the pineapple chunks and cashew nuts and mix well once more.

- Transfer the sweet and sour chicken stir-fry to a serving plate and serve with Jasmine Rice (pages 142 and 144).

CHICKEN PINEAPPLE STIR-FRY –
GAI PAD SAPPAROD

Serves 1–2

1 generous tablespoon tomato ketchup
2 teaspoons Tamarind Paste (page 188)
Dash of thin soy sauce
Dash of fish sauce
½ teaspoon sriracha sauce
1 teaspoon sweet chilli sauce
Dash of rice wine vinegar
½ teaspoon caster sugar
75ml light chicken stock
1 tablespoon vegetable oil
2 garlic cloves, roughly chopped
150g Marinated Stir-Fry Chicken Thighs (page 63)
1 small onion, roughly chopped
3 cherry tomatoes, halved
1 handful pineapple chunks, fresh or from a tin (about
    75g drained weight)
Pinch of coriander powder
Pinch of black pepper
1 spring onion, thinly sliced
Small handful fresh coriander, roughly chopped

- Put the tomato ketchup, tamarind paste, thin soy sauce, fish sauce, sriracha sauce, sweet chilli sauce, rice wine vinegar, caster sugar and light chicken stock in a bowl. Mix well and set aside.

- Heat a wok or large frying pan over a medium heat. Add the vegetable oil and garlic and stir-fry for 30–40 seconds until aromatic. Add the marinated chicken thighs. Let the chicken sit in the pan for 20 seconds then stir-fry for 2 minutes until browned. Add the onion, cherry tomatoes, pineapple chunks, coriander powder and black pepper and stir-fry for 1 minute.

- Add the prepared sauce and mix well. Stir-fry for 2–3 minutes until the sauce reduces slightly.

- Transfer the chicken and pineapple stir-fry to a serving plate, garnish with spring onion and fresh coriander and serve with Jasmine Rice (pages 142 and 144).

GARLIC AND PEPPER PRAWNS STIR-FRY
– GOONG TOD KRATIEM PRIK THAI

Serves 1–2

1 tablespoon oyster sauce
2 teaspoons thin soy sauce
½ teaspoon thick soy sauce
Dash of fish sauce
½ teaspoon caster sugar
75ml light stock or water
1 tablespoon vegetable oil
Pinch of salt
2 pinches of white pepper
125g raw king prawns
Generous pinch of black pepper
2 teaspoons Crispy Fried Garlic (page 172)
Small handful fresh coriander leaves, roughly chopped

- Put the oyster sauce, thin soy sauce, thick soy sauce, fish
  sauce, caster sugar and light stock or water in a bowl. Mix
  well and set aside.

- Put the pinch of salt and 1 pinch of white pepper in a bowl.
  Add the king prawns and mix well. Cover and set aside for
  5 minutes.

- Heat a wok or large frying pan over a medium-high heat. Add the vegetable oil and marinated king prawns. Let the prawns sit in the pan for 20 seconds then stir-fry for 1–2 minutes until pink.

- Add the prepared sauce and mix well. Add the black and remaining white pepper and stir-fry for 1–2 minutes, until the sauce reduces slightly.

- Transfer the garlic and black pepper prawns stir-fry to a serving plate, garnish with crispy fried garlic and fresh coriander, and serve with Jasmine Rice (pages 142 and 144).

CHICKEN AND GINGER STIR-FRY –
GAI PAD KHING

Serves 1–2

1 tablespoon oyster sauce
2 teaspoons thin soy sauce
1 teaspoon fish sauce
½ teaspoon palm sugar
Pinch of white pepper
75ml light stock or water
125–150g Marinated Stir-Fry Chicken Breast (page 62)
1 tablespoon vegetable oil
2 garlic cloves, finely chopped
1 inch (2.5cm) piece of fresh ginger, roughly chopped
    (about the same size as 2 garlic cloves)
1 small onion, sliced
¼ red pepper, sliced
1 spring onion, sliced

- Put the oyster sauce, thin soy sauce, fish sauce, palm sugar, white pepper and light stock or water in a bowl. Mix well and set aside.

- Fill a saucepan with water and bring to the boil. Carefully drop the marinated chicken into the boiling water and simmer for 1 minute until sealed. Drain and set aside.

- Heat a wok or large frying pan over a medium heat. Add the chopped garlic and ginger and stir-fry for 20–30 seconds until aromatic. Add the marinated chicken, onion and red pepper and stir-fry for 1 minute.

- Add the prepared sauce and mix well. Stir-fry for a further 1 minute, or until the sauce is slightly reduced. Add the spring onion and mix through.

- Transfer the chicken and ginger stir-fry to a serving plate and serve with Jasmine Rice (pages 142 and 144).

PORK AND HOLY BASIL STIR-FRY –
PAD KRA PAO MOO

My favourite Thai dish!

Serves 1–2

1 small shallot, finely chopped
3 garlic cloves, roughly chopped
2–3 red bird's-eye chillies, thinly sliced
1 teaspoon oyster sauce
1 teaspoon light soy sauce
Dash of dark soy sauce
Dash of fish sauce
½ teaspoon palm sugar
1 tablespoon vegetable oil
100–125g pork mince
Small handful green beans, sliced
75ml light stock or water
Handful fresh basil leaves (see note on page 13)

- Put the shallot, garlic and chillies in a pestle and mortar. Pound to a rough paste. Set aside.

- Put the oyster sauce, light soy sauce, dark soy sauce, fish sauce and sugar in a bowl. Mix well and set aside.

- Heat the oil in a wok or large frying pan over a medium-high heat. Add the pork mince and stir-fry for 1 minute. Add the sliced green beans and the prepared chillies, shallot and garlic mix. Stir-fry for a further minute.

- Add the prepared sauce and light stock or water and mix through. Cook for 1–2 minutes until the sauce reaches your preferred consistency.

- Switch off the heat, add the basil and mix through for 30 seconds.

- Transfer the pad kra pao moo to a serving plate and serve with steamed Jasmine Rice (see pages 142 and 144), Crispy Fried Egg (page 192) and some fresh cucumber slices.

PORK AND RED CURRY STIR-FRY –
PAD PRIK GAENG MOO

Serves 1–2

1 tablespoon vegetable oil
1 tablespoon Red Curry Paste (page 179, or from a tub)
125–150g Marinated Stir-Fry Pork (page 60)
1 teaspoon thin soy sauce
Dash fish sauce
½ teaspoon palm sugar or light brown sugar
1 makrut lime leaf
2 tablespoons light stock or water
1 mild red chilli, sliced

- Heat a wok or large frying pan over a medium heat. Add the vegetable oil and red curry paste and stir-fry for 1 minute until the paste is sizzling and aromatic. Add the marinated pork and stir-fry for 1–2 minutes until browned. Add the thin soy sauce, fish sauce, sugar and makrut lime leaf. Add the light stock or water and stir-fry for 1–2 minutes until the sauce reaches your preferred consistency.

- Transfer the pork and red curry stir-fry to a serving plate, garnish with red chilli and serve with Jasmine Rice (pages 142 and 144).

CURRIES AND SLOW COOKS

I n contrast to the speed and instant satisfaction provided by stir-fry dishes, this chapter includes recipes for curry dishes that tick along slowly, building depth of flavour and tenderising meats in the process. Rich and indulgent with coconut milk, Thai curries are packed full of aromatic and flavourful ingredients, and although the initial cooking process may be a little more time-consuming, the rewards are plentiful.

CHICKEN RED CURRY – GAENG PHED GAI

Serves 1–2

200ml coconut milk

1 heaped tablespoon Red Curry Paste (page 179, or from a tub – about 20g)

125–150g skinless, boneless chicken thigh fillets, cut into bite-sized pieces

75ml water

2 makrut lime leaves, torn in half

Small handful tinned bamboo shoots, rinsed and drained (80g drained weight)

1 teaspoon fish sauce

1 teaspoon palm sugar or light brown sugar

Small handful fresh basil leaves (see note on page 13)

½ mild red chilli, sliced

- Heat a wok or saucepan over a medium heat. Add 75ml of the coconut milk, bring to the boil and add the red curry paste. Reduce the heat to low and stir-fry the curry paste and coconut milk together for 1–2 minutes until aromatic. Add the chicken thighs and mix well.

- Add the remaining coconut milk, water and lime leaves. Simmer for around 30 minutes until the chicken is cooked and the sauce has slightly reduced. Add the bamboo shoots and simmer for 1 minute.

- Add the fish sauce and sugar and mix well. Simmer for another minute then transfer the red curry to a serving plate. Garnish with fresh basil and sliced chilli, and serve with Jasmine Rice (pages 142 and 144).

BEEF MASSAMAN CURRY –
GAENG MASSAMAN NEUA

Serves 1–2

200ml coconut milk

1 generous tablespoon Massaman Curry Paste (page 181,
   or from a tub – about 20g)

75ml water

200g diced stewing steak

1 onion, roughly chopped

1 carrot, sliced

1 potato, cut into 6 pieces

Dash of fish sauce

1 teaspoon palm sugar

½ teaspoon Tamarind Paste (page 188)

Small handful fried cashew nuts (page 176)

- Heat a wok or saucepan over a medium heat. Add 75ml of
  the coconut milk, bring to the boil and add the massaman
  curry paste. Reduce the heat to low and stir-fry the curry
  paste and coconut milk together for 1–2 minutes until
  aromatic.

- Add the remaining coconut milk, water and diced beef,
  cover with a lid and simmer for 2½ hours, stirring
  occasionally.

- Add the onion, carrot and potato and simmer for a further 30–40 minutes until the beef is tender, the vegetables are soft and the curry sauce is slightly thickened.

- Add the fish sauce, palm sugar and tamarind paste and mix well. Add the fried cashews, mix once more and transfer the beef massaman curry to a serving plate. Serve with Jasmine Rice (pages 142 and 144).

GREEN CURRY – GAENG KHIAO WAAN GAI

Serves 1–2

200ml coconut milk

1 heaped tablespoon Green Curry Paste (page 186, or
from a tub – about 20g)

150g skinless, boneless chicken thigh fillets, cut into bite-
sized pieces

125ml light chicken stock

2 makrut lime leaves, torn in half

Small handful tinned bamboo shoots, rinsed and drained
(80g drained weight)

2 teaspoons fish sauce

1 tablespoon palm sugar

Small handful fresh basil leaves (see note on page 13)

½ mild red chilli, sliced

- Heat a wok or saucepan over a medium heat. Add 75ml of
the coconut milk, bring to the boil and add the green curry
paste. Reduce the heat to low and stir-fry the curry paste
and coconut milk together for 1–2 minutes until aromatic.
Add the chicken thighs and mix well.

- Add the remaining coconut milk, light chicken stock and
lime leaves. Simmer for around 30 minutes until the
chicken is cooked and the sauce has slightly reduced. Add
the bamboo shoots and simmer for 1 minute.

- Add the fish sauce and palm sugar and mix well. Simmer for another minute then transfer the green curry to a serving plate. Garnish with fresh basil and sliced chilli and serve with Jasmine Rice (pages 142 and 144).

PANANG PORK CURRY – GAENG PANANG MOO

Serves 1–2

125ml coconut milk

1½ tablespoons Panang Curry Paste (page 184, or from a tub)

150g pork tenderloin fillet, sliced

Dash of fish sauce

1 teaspoon sugar

1 makrut lime leaf, thinly sliced

½ mild red chilli, sliced

- Heat a wok or saucepan over a medium heat. Add the coconut milk and curry paste and mix well. Once the mix begins to simmer, reduce the heat to low and simmer for 5 minutes. Add the sliced pork, fish sauce and sugar, mix well once more and simmer for 10 minutes, or until the pork is cooked through and tender.

- Transfer the panang curry to a serving bowl, garnish with lime leaf and red chilli and serve with Jasmine Rice (pages 142 and 144).

CHICKEN JUNGLE CURRY – GAENG PA GAI

As the name implies, this dish traditionally made use of the freshest and most available items found in the forests of Thailand. In keeping with that attitude, you can make the most of whichever meats or vegetables you have in the fridge to make this hot curry dish. The absence of coconut milk makes for a more direct delivery of heat, the impact of the fresh chillies and curry paste left undiluted.

Serves 1–2

1 tablespoon vegetable oil

2 teaspoons Red Curry Paste (page 179, or from a tub)

1 red bird's-eye chilli, thinly sliced

125–150g skinless, boneless chicken thigh fillets, cut into bite-sized pieces

275ml light stock or water

2 makrut lime leaves

1 small stem green peppercorns, or 1 teaspoon pickled green peppercorns

1 carrot, thinly sliced

4 green beans, sliced

2 mushrooms, sliced

Small handful tinned bamboo shoots, rinsed and drained (about 20g drained weight)

1 teaspoon fish sauce

1 teaspoon fresh lime juice

½ teaspoon palm sugar or light brown sugar
Small handful fresh basil leaves (see note on page 13)
Small handful fresh coriander leaves, roughly chopped

- Heat a wok or large saucepan over a medium heat. Add the vegetable oil, red curry paste and fresh chilli and stir-fry for 20–30 seconds until aromatic. Add the chicken thighs and mix well.

- Add the light stock or water, lime leaves, green peppercorns, carrot, green beans, mushrooms and bamboo shoots. Mix well, bring to the boil, reduce the heat to low and simmer for 5–6 minutes.

- Add the fish sauce, lime juice and sugar. Mix well, add the basil leaves and mix once more. Transfer the jungle curry to a serving bowl, garnish with fresh coriander and serve with Jasmine Rice (pages 142 and 144).

SOUTHERN THAI-STYLE PORK BELLY STEW – MOO HONG

Serves 3–4

1 tablespoon oyster sauce
2 teaspoons thin soy sauce
1 teaspoon thick soy sauce
1 teaspoon sweet soy sauce
1 teaspoon palm sugar or light brown sugar
Pinch of white pepper
1 shallot, finely chopped
2 garlic cloves, finely chopped
1 teaspoon fresh coriander stems, thinly sliced
250g pork belly slices, cut into bite-sized pieces
225ml light stock or water
1 star anise
1 spring onion, thinly sliced
Small handful fresh coriander leaves, finely chopped

- Put the oyster sauce, thin soy sauce, thick soy sauce, sweet soy sauce, sugar and white pepper in a bowl. Mix briefly and set aside.

- Put the shallot, garlic and fresh coriander stems in a pestle and mortar. Pound to a rough paste. Transfer the paste to a small bowl and set aside.

- Heat a saucepan over a medium heat. Add the pork belly and fry for 5 minutes, or until browned on all sides. Drain off any excess fat if desired. Add the prepared garlic, chilli and coriander and stir-fry for 30–40 seconds until fragrant.

- Add the prepared sauce and mix well. Add the stock or water and star anise, mix once more and simmer for 1 hour and 20 minutes, stirring occasionally until the pork is tender and the sauce is reduced.

- Remove the star anise. Transfer the pork belly stew to a serving bowl, garnish with spring onion and fresh coriander and serve with steamed Jasmine Rice (pages 142 and 144).

SOUPS AND SALADS

Cooked with aromatic ingredients including garlic, galangal, lemongrass and lime leaves, Thai soups are full of flavour. With the added comfort of coconut milk, the experience is one to make you feel soothed and satisfied.

Thai salads are intensely flavourful, with spicy chilli, refreshing and sour lime juice and savoury fish sauce, as well as abundant use of fresh herbs. Often combining savoury and sweet ingredients, these dishes are perfect as part of a larger meal, and substantial enough to be enjoyed with a side of Sticky Rice (see pages 150 and 151) or fresh lettuce leaves.

GLASS NOODLE SOUP – GAENG JUED WOON SEN

Serves 1–2

1 x 50g nest vermicelli bean threads
75g minced chicken
1 teaspoon oyster sauce
2 garlic cloves, finely chopped
1 teaspoon fresh coriander stems, thinly sliced
1 teaspoon vegetable oil
325ml light stock or water
1 teaspoon fish sauce
Dash of thin soy sauce
Pinch of caster sugar
Pinch of white pepper
1 spring onion, thinly sliced
Small handful fresh coriander leaves, roughly chopped

- Put the vermicelli bean threads in a bowl. Cover with boiling water and soak for 5 minutes, stirring once or twice until the noodles are softened. Drain, rinse briefly with cold water, drain once more, cut the noodles into smaller pieces and set aside.

- Put the minced chicken and oyster sauce in a separate bowl. Mix well and set aside.

- Put the garlic and fresh coriander stems in a pestle and mortar. Pound to a rough paste. Transfer the paste to a small bowl and set aside.

- Heat the oil in a saucepan over a medium heat. Add the prepared paste and stir-fry for 20–30 seconds until aromatic. Add the light stock or water, fish sauce, thin soy sauce, caster sugar and white pepper. Bring to the boil, reduce the heat to low and simmer for 5 minutes. Form small meatballs with the prepared chicken mix and carefully drop into the simmering soup. Simmer for 2 minutes until the chicken is cooked.

- Transfer the glass noodle soup to a serving bowl. Garnish with spring onion and fresh coriander and serve.

PORK AND RICE SOUP – KHAO TOM MOO SAP

Serves 1–2

1 small shallot, finely chopped
1 garlic clove, finely chopped
1 teaspoon fresh coriander stems, finely chopped
1 red bird's-eye chilli, thinly sliced (optional)
75g pork mince
1 teaspoon oyster sauce
1 teaspoon coconut oil or vegetable oil
½ carrot, cut into thin matchsticks
½ lemongrass stalk, bashed with a rolling pin
1 inch (2.5cm) piece of galangal
325ml light chicken stock
50g cooked Jasmine Rice (pages 142 and 144)
1 teaspoon fish sauce
½ teaspoon thin soy sauce
Pinch of white pepper
1 teaspoon fresh lime juice
1 spring onion, thinly sliced
Small handful fresh coriander leaves, roughly chopped

- Put the shallot, garlic, coriander stems and red chilli in a pestle and mortar. Pound to a rough paste. Transfer the paste to a small bowl and set aside.

- Put the pork mince and oyster sauce in a bowl. Mix well and set aside.

- Heat the oil in a saucepan over a medium heat. Add the prepared paste and stir-fry for 20–30 seconds. Add the carrot, lemongrass, galangal and light chicken stock. Bring to the boil, reduce the heat to low and simmer for 5 minutes. Form small meatballs with the prepared pork mix and carefully drop into the simmering soup. Simmer for 1 minute.

- Add the cooked rice and mix well. Simmer for 2 minutes. Add the fish sauce, thin soy sauce, white pepper and lime juice and mix once more.

- Transfer the pork and rice soup into a serving bowl. Garnish with spring onion and fresh coriander and serve.

PRAWN HOT AND SOUR SOUP
– TOM YUM GOONG

Serves 1–2

1 shallot, finely chopped

2 garlic cloves, finely chopped

¼ inch (0.6cm) piece of galangal (about the size of 1 garlic clove)

1–2 red bird's-eye chillies, thinly sliced

1 teaspoon vegetable oil

325ml light stock or water

1 lemongrass stalk (white part only), bashed with a rolling pin

1 makrut lime leaf, torn in half

75g king prawns

2 small button mushrooms, sliced

4 cherry tomatoes, halved

2 tablespoons evaporated milk

2 teaspoons Chilli Paste (page 163)

1 teaspoon fish sauce

Dash of thin soy sauce

1 teaspoon Tamarind Paste (page 188)

1 teaspoon fresh lime juice

Small handful fresh coriander leaves

- Put the shallot, garlic, galangal and chillies in a pestle and mortar. Pound to a rough paste. Transfer the paste to a small bowl and set aside.

- Heat the oil in a saucepan. Add the prepared paste and stir-fry for 20–30 seconds until aromatic. Add the light stock, lemongrass and lime leaf. Bring to the boil, reduce the heat to low and simmer for 2 minutes. Add the king prawns, mushrooms and tomatoes and simmer for 2 minutes.

- Add the evaporated milk, chilli paste, fish sauce, thin soy sauce and tamarind paste. Mix well and simmer for 1 minute.

- Pour the tom yum soup into a serving bowl. Add the fresh lime juice, garnish with fresh coriander and serve.

CHICKEN SOUP WITH GALANGAL
– TOM KHA GAI

Serves 1–2

1 garlic clove, finely chopped

¼ inch (0.6cm) piece of galangal, finely chopped (about the size of 1 garlic clove)

1 lemongrass stalk (white part only), thinly sliced

1 red bird's-eye chilli, thinly sliced

1 teaspoon vegetable oil

225ml light chicken stock or water

75g skinless, boneless chicken thighs, thinly sliced

125ml coconut milk

1 makrut lime leaf

2 small button mushrooms, sliced

4 cherry tomatoes, halved

1 teaspoon fish sauce

Dash of thin soy sauce

½ teaspoon palm sugar or light brown sugar

1 teaspoon lime juice

1 spring onion, sliced

Small handful fresh coriander leaves, roughly chopped

- Put the garlic, galangal, lemongrass and chilli in a pestle and mortar. Pound to a rough paste. Transfer the paste to a small bowl and set aside.

- Heat the oil in a saucepan. Add the prepared paste and stir-fry for 20–30 seconds until aromatic. Add the light stock or water, chicken thighs, coconut milk and lime leaf. Bring to the boil, reduce the heat to low and simmer for 10 minutes. Add the mushrooms and tomatoes. Mix well and simmer for 1 minute. Add the fish sauce, thin soy sauce and sugar. Mix well and simmer for a further minute.

- Pour the tom kha gai soup into a serving bowl. Add the fresh lime juice, garnish with spring onion and fresh coriander and serve.

CURRY CHICKEN NOODLE SOUP – KHAO SOI GAI

If you'd like to save a cooking step, you can buy packs of fried crispy noodles in Chinese supermarkets. Alternatively – albeit much less traditionally – a handful of ramen noodles straight from the packet crushed over the top of the soup adds an equally delicious crunchy texture.

Serves 1–2

1 x large nest dried egg noodles (about 110g dried weight)
125ml coconut milk
2 teaspoons Massaman Curry Paste (page 181) or Red Curry Paste (page 179)
¼ teaspoon turmeric
2 skin-on, bone-in chicken drumsticks
175ml light chicken stock
Vegetable oil for deep-frying
1 teaspoon fish sauce
Dash of thin soy sauce
½ teaspoon palm sugar or light brown sugar
1 teaspoon fresh lime juice
1 spring onion, thinly sliced
Small handful fresh coriander leaves, roughly chopped

Additional toppings (optional)
Hard-boiled egg
Pickled mustard greens
Lime wedges

- Break a fistful from the block of dried egg noodles and set aside. Put the remaining dried egg noodles in a large heat-safe bowl, cover with boiling water and stir briefly. Set aside for 2 minutes, or until the noodles are soft. Drain, rinse with cold water, drain once more and set aside.

- Put half of the coconut milk in a large saucepan over a medium heat. Once the coconut milk is sizzling, add the massaman or red curry paste and turmeric and stir-fry for 30–40 seconds until aromatic. Add the chicken drumsticks and stir-fry for 1 minute. Add the remaining coconut milk and light chicken stock. Bring to the boil, reduce the heat to low, cover with a lid and simmer for 30–40 minutes until the chicken drumsticks are cooked through.

- Heat the oil for deep-frying to 180°C/350°F. Add the reserved chunk of dried noodles and fry for 2–3 minutes until crispy. Remove from the oil with a slotted spoon and set aside.

- Add the fish sauce, thin soy sauce and sugar to the simmering soup. Mix well and simmer for a further minute.

- Arrange the soft noodles in a large soup bowl. Ladle the curry soup and chicken into the bowl. Add the fresh lime juice and top with the crispy fried noodles. Garnish with spring onion and fresh coriander. Serve with your choice of additional toppings.

MIXED SALAD WITH PEANUT DRESSING

At Topaz Thai in New Jersey, Mama welcomes you to the restaurant with a complimentary bowl of this delicious fresh salad.

Serves 1–2

2 tablespoons smooth peanut butter (about 30g)
2 teaspoons sweet chilli sauce
½ teaspoon thin soy sauce
½ teaspoon garlic ginger paste
1 teaspoon rice wine vinegar
2 teaspoons fresh lime juice
Dash of sesame oil
1 carrot, thinly sliced
Small handful napa cabbage leaves, roughly chopped
Small handful red cabbage leaves, thinly sliced
1 teaspoon unsalted roasted peanuts (page 177), ground
    or pounded in a pestle and mortar (about 2g)

- Put the smooth peanut butter, sweet chilli sauce, thin soy sauce, garlic ginger paste, rice wine vinegar, fresh lime juice and sesame oil in a bowl. Whisk thoroughly until well combined. Alternatively, you can add the ingredients to a food-safe container with a well-fitting lid and shake well until combined.

- Arrange the carrot and cabbage leaves in a bowl. Add the peanut dressing to taste and toss gently. Arrange the dressed salad in a serving bowl, garnish with peanuts and serve.

THE THAI TAKEAWAY SECRET

GRILLED CHICKEN SALAD – YUM GAI YANG

Despite the name, the star of this dish is a super-crispy, deep-fried, panko-coated chicken breast fillet.

Serves 1–2

1 large skinless, boneless chicken breast fillet (about 150g)
¼ teaspoon sea salt
Pinch of white pepper
2 tablespoons plain flour
1 egg
8 tablespoons panko breadcrumbs
Oil for deep-frying
1 salad tomato, thinly sliced
1 handful lettuce leaves, roughly chopped
¼ cucumber, thinly sliced

- Place the chicken breast on a large piece of greaseproof paper. Cover with another layer of greaseproof paper and use a meat hammer or heavy rolling pin to pound the chicken flat, to around 5mm (¼ inch) thick. Season with the salt and pepper.

- Spread the plain flour on a plate, whisk the egg in a bowl and arrange the panko breadcrumbs on a separate plate. Keeping one hand dry, drip the chicken into the plain flour, then into the egg mix and finally into the panko breadcrumbs, patting down firmly to ensure the chicken is fully coated.

- Heat the oil for deep-frying to 180°C/350°F. Carefully drop the breaded chicken breast into the hot oil and fry for 3–4 minutes, turning once or twice until the chicken is cooked through and the breading is golden and crispy. Remove from the oil with a slotted spoon, drain off any excess oil and set aside on a chopping board to rest for 2 minutes.

- Arrange the tomato, lettuce and cucumber on a serving plate. Slice the crispy chicken and arrange on top of the salad. Serve with Sweet Chilli Sauce (page 169).

PAPAYA SALAD – SOM TAM

Serves 1–2

1½ tablespoons fish sauce

2 tablespoons fresh lime juice

2 tablespoons palm sugar or light brown sugar

4 garlic cloves, finely chopped

2 red Thai chillies, finely chopped

2 teaspoons dried shrimp

1 carrot, cut into thin matchsticks or grated

8 green beans, cut into small pieces

2 tablespoons roasted peanuts (page 177)

6 cherry tomatoes, halved

1 papaya, shredded

2–3 fresh lime wedges

- Put the fish sauce, lime juice and sugar in a bowl. Mix well and set aside.

- Put the garlic, chillies and dried shrimp in a pestle and mortar. Pound to a fine paste. Add the carrot and green beans and half of the roasted peanuts. Pound briefly for 20–30 seconds. Add the tomatoes and pound once or twice more. Transfer the ingredients in the pestle and mortar to a large bowl.

- Put the papaya in the pestle and mortar and pound once or twice. Transfer the papaya to the bowl with the other ingredients. Add the prepared sauce and mix well. Transfer the papaya salad to a serving plate, garnish with the remaining roasted peanuts and serve with lime wedges.

PORK SALAD – LARB MOO

Serves 1–2

1 teaspoon thin soy sauce
1 teaspoon fish sauce
1 tablespoon fresh lime juice
½ teaspoon sugar
2 shallots, thinly sliced
1 spring onion, thinly sliced
Small handful fresh coriander leaves, finely chopped
Small handful fresh mint leaves, finely chopped
1 generous tablespoon Toasted Rice (page 178)
1 teaspoon Roasted Chilli Flakes (or to taste; page 171)
125g pork mince
3 tablespoons water

- Put the thin soy sauce, fish sauce, lime juice and sugar in a bowl. Mix well and set aside.

- Put the shallots, spring onion, coriander, mint, toasted rice and chilli flakes in a separate large bowl. Set aside.

- Heat a saucepan, wok or frying pan over a medium-high heat. Add the pork mince and water and stir-fry for 3–4 minutes until the water is absorbed and the pork is cooked.

- Switch off the heat and allow the pork mix to stand for 1 minute. Add the prepared sauce, vegetables and herbs. Mix well once more and transfer the pork salad to a serving plate. Serve with Sticky Rice (see pages 150 and 151) and/ or fresh lettuce leaves.

INSTANT NOODLE SALAD – YUM MAMA

Serves 1–2

1 jumbo packet Mama instant noodles (90g)

1 garlic clove, finely chopped

1 red bird's-eye chilli, thinly sliced

1 teaspoon fresh coriander stems, finely chopped

1 teaspoon fish sauce

Dash of thin soy sauce

1 tablespoon fresh lime juice

1 teaspoon palm sugar

1 shallot, thinly sliced

1 carrot, cut into thin matchsticks

1 spring onion, thinly sliced

Small handful fresh coriander leaves, finely chopped

1–2 cabbage leaves, roughly chopped

1 teaspoon vegetable oil

125g pork mince

- Open the instant noodles and separate the dry noodle block from the seasoning sachets. Set aside.

- Put the garlic, chilli and fresh coriander stems in a pestle and mortar. Pound to a rough paste. Transfer to a large bowl and add the fish sauce, soy sauce, lime juice, sugar and 1 teaspoon of each noodle seasoning sachet. Add the shallot, carrot, spring onion and fresh coriander.

- Fill a saucepan with water and bring to the boil. When the water is boiling, add the dry noodle nest and cabbage leaves and simmer for 1–2 minutes until the noodles become soft and can be stirred with a fork. Strain the water and set the cooked noodles and cabbage aside.

- Heat the vegetable oil in a frying pan over a medium-high heat. Add the pork mince and stir-fry for 3–4 minutes until well browned, sizzling and cooked through.

- Combine the cooked noodles and the prepared salad. Top with the fried pork mince and mix thoroughly. Add more lime juice, sugar or seasoning from the noodle sachets to taste and serve.

CHEF'S SPECIALS

With such a variety of flavours, ingredients and dishes offered up by Thai takeaway chefs, you're certain to find a few favourites that keep you coming back for more. In truth, whatever day you corner me on, my list of chosen chart-toppers is bound to be different – that being said, this chapter includes recipes for a few dishes that I'd definitely recommend.

Thai-style omelette (khai jiao) fried indulgently in a generous amount of hot oil is such a tasty treat that you'll consider it every time you prepare a plate of rice, while the classic green curry is positively bursting with fresh flavours.

For added virtue when preparing a selection of dishes, mixed vegetables in oyster sauce are deliciously savoury and slightly sweet, while Thai fried chicken may very well argue its case for being one of the finest takes on a dish beloved worldwide.

MIXED VEGETABLES IN OYSTER SAUCE – PAD PAK RUAM

Serves 1–2

1 tablespoon oyster sauce
1 teaspoon thin soy sauce
1 teaspoon thick soy sauce
Dash of fish sauce
¼ teaspoon caster sugar
50ml light stock or water
1 tablespoon vegetable oil
1 onion, roughly chopped
1 carrot, thinly sliced
2 button mushrooms, quartered
½ red pepper, roughly chopped
½ green pepper, roughly chopped
Small handful tinned bamboo shoots, rinsed and drained
    (80g drained weight)
1 generous teaspoon garlic oil (page 172)
Pinch of white pepper
Small handful fresh coriander leaves, roughly chopped

- Put the oyster sauce, thin soy sauce, thick soy sauce, fish sauce, caster sugar and light stock or water in a bowl. Mix well and set aside.

- Heat a wok or large frying pan over a medium-high heat. Add the vegetable oil, onion, carrot, mushrooms, red pepper, green pepper, bamboo shoots and garlic oil. Stir-fry for 1 minute.

- Add the prepared sauce and mix well. Add the white pepper and stir-fry for 1–2 minutes, until the sauce reduces slightly. Transfer to a serving plate, garnish with fresh coriander and serve with Jasmine Rice (pages 142 and 144).

THAI-STYLE OMELETTE – KHAI JIAO

Thai omelettes are cooked in generous amounts of oil until they are nicely browned. If desired, add 60g pork mince to the egg mix to make a Thai-style pork omelette (khai jiao moo sab).

Serves 1

2 eggs
½ teaspoon oyster sauce
Dash of thin soy sauce
Dash of fish sauce
Pinch of white pepper
Pinch of black pepper
1 teaspoon water
1 spring onion, sliced
3 tablespoons vegetable oil

- Put the eggs, oyster sauce, thin soy sauce, fish sauce, white pepper, black pepper, water and spring onion in a bowl. Whisk thoroughly and set aside.

- Heat the oil in a small wok over a medium-high heat. When the oil is hot, whisk the eggs again for a few seconds, hold the bowl above the oil and carefully pour the egg mix into the pan. The egg mix will sizzle and puff up immediately. Cook for 30–40 seconds, or until the edges begin to crisp, then flip the omelette with a spatula and cook for a further 30–40 seconds, or until nicely browned on both sides.

- Transfer the cooked omelette to a serving plate and serve with Jasmine Rice (pages 142 and 144), Chilli Paste (page 163) and sweet soy sauce.

MAMA'S CRISPY VOLCANO CHICKEN

Over several trips to New Jersey I was served this deliciously sweet and slightly spicy dish by Mama at Topaz Thai. I hope this recipe does justice to her sensationally good cooking skills!

Serves 1–2

2 tablespoons oyster sauce
1 teaspoon thin soy sauce
1 teaspoon thick soy sauce
Dash of fish sauce
1 tablespoon Tamarind Paste (page 188)
1 tablespoon sweet chilli sauce
Pinch of white pepper
75ml light stock or water
1 tablespoon vegetable oil
1 onion, roughly chopped
½ carrot, thinly sliced
1 portion cooked crispy chicken (page 65)
1–2 pak choi leaves, roughly chopped
Small handful fresh coriander leaves, roughly chopped

- Put the oyster sauce, thin soy sauce, thick soy sauce, fish sauce, tamarind paste, sweet chilli sauce, white pepper and light stock or water in a bowl. Mix well and set aside.

- Heat a wok or large frying pan over a medium-high heat. Add the vegetable oil, onion and carrot. Stir-fry for 1 minute.

- Add the prepared sauce and mix well. Stir-fry for 1–2 minutes, until the sauce reduces slightly. Add the cooked crispy chicken and pak choi leaves and stir-fry for 30 seconds. Transfer the crispy volcano chicken to a serving plate, garnish with fresh coriander and serve with Jasmine Rice (pages 142 and 144).

THAI FRIED CHICKEN – GAI TOD

This lightly spiced crispy chicken is delicious served piping hot, and leftovers will keep well in the fridge for two days for snacking – if it lasts that long!

Serves 4–6

900g skinless, boneless chicken thigh fillets
1 teaspoon cumin powder
½ teaspoon garlic powder
Pinch of galangal powder (optional)
Pinch of turmeric
½ teaspoon black pepper
¼ teaspoon white pepper
1 teaspoon thin soy sauce
Dash of fish sauce
1 egg
Oil for deep-frying
250g plain flour

- Cut each chicken thigh fillet into two equal pieces and place in a large bowl. Add the cumin powder, garlic powder, galangal powder (if using), turmeric, black pepper, white pepper, thin soy sauce and fish sauce. Mix well and set aside for 5 minutes.

- Add the egg to the prepared chicken and mix well.

- Heat the oil for deep-frying to 180°C/350°F. Put the plain flour in a bowl. Working in batches, press some of the chicken thigh pieces into the flour, mixing well and pressing down hard until the chicken is fully coated. Carefully drop the coated chicken pieces into the hot oil and fry for about 6–8 minutes, or until just cooked through and golden. Use a slotted spoon to remove the fried chicken from the oil, drain off any excess oil and set aside on a plate. Repeat the process until all the chicken pieces are coated and cooked.

- Arrange the fried chicken pieces on serving plate and serve with Sweet Chilli Sauce (page 169).

CRYING TIGER STEAK – SUEA RONG HAI

In times gone by, it was said that this dish was so named due to the use of cuts of meat so tough that even a tiger couldn't chew them. Others attribute its name to the sight of fat dripping from the meat, resembling tears as it cooks on the grill.

Serves 1–2

1 generous tablespoon oyster sauce
2 teaspoons thin soy sauce
1 teaspoon fish sauce
1 teaspoon fresh lime juice
Pinch of black pepper
1 teaspoon palm sugar
½ teaspoon smoked garlic powder (optional)
1 rib-eye steak, roughly 225g
1 tablespoon vegetable oil
Small handful fresh coriander leaves, roughly chopped

- Put the oyster sauce, thin soy sauce, fish sauce, lime juice, black pepper and palm sugar in a wide bowl. Add the smoked garlic powder if desired – I like the smoky flavour it provides, especially when cooking inside where the additional flavour provided by an outdoor grill isn't available.

- Add the steak and mix well until fully coated. Cover and set aside in the fridge for 1 hour, or overnight. Remove the marinated steak from the fridge 20 minutes before you want to cook, add the vegetable oil and mix briefly.

- Heat a griddle pan or large frying pan over a medium-high heat. When the pan is hot, add the marinated steak and fry for 1 minute on each side. Reduce the heat to medium and continue cooking for another 1 minute (medium-rare), 2 minutes (medium) or 3 minutes (medium–well done), turning every minute as the steak cooks. Transfer the steak to a plate, cover loosely with tinfoil and let it rest for 3–4 minutes.

- Slice the steak across the grain and arrange on a serving plate. Garnish with fresh coriander leaves and serve with Spicy Dipping Sauce (page 165).

CRISPY PRAWNS IN SWEET CHILLI TAMARIND SAUCE – GOONG MA KHAM

Serves 1–2

2 tablespoons oyster sauce
1 teaspoon thin soy sauce
1 teaspoon thick soy sauce
Dash of fish sauce
1 tablespoon Tamarind Paste (page 188)
1 tablespoon sweet chilli sauce
Pinch of white pepper
75ml light stock or water
1 tablespoon vegetable oil
1 shallot, roughly chopped
2 garlic cloves, roughly chopped
1 portion cooked crispy king prawns (page 64)
Small handful fresh coriander leaves, roughly chopped
½ mild red chilli, thinly sliced (optional)

- Put the oyster sauce, thin soy sauce, thick soy sauce, fish sauce, tamarind paste, sweet chilli sauce, white pepper and light stock or water in a bowl. Mix well and set aside.

- Heat a wok or large frying pan over a medium-high heat. Add the vegetable oil, shallot and garlic and stir-fry for 30–40 seconds until aromatic.

- Add the prepared sauce and mix well. Stir-fry for 1–2 minutes, until the sauce reduces slightly. Add the cooked crispy king prawns and stir-fry for 30 seconds.

- Transfer the crispy prawns in sweet chilli tamarind sauce to a serving plate. Garnish with fresh coriander leaves and fresh chilli if desired and serve with Jasmine Rice (pages 142 and 144).

STEAMED SEA BASS – PLA
KRAPONG NEUNG MANAO

If you have some lemongrass stalks you can steam the fish fillets on top of them for added flavour.

Serves 1–2

2 teaspoons palm sugar
2 tablespoons water
2 teaspoons fish sauce
1 tablespoon fresh lime juice
3 garlic cloves, finely chopped
1 red bird's-eye chilli, thinly sliced
2 sea bass fillets
Small handful fresh coriander leaves, roughly chopped

- Put the palm sugar and water in a small microwave-safe bowl. Heat on full power for 10 seconds and mix well until the sugar is dissolved. Add the fish sauce, fresh lime juice, garlic and red chilli. Mix well and set aside.

- Steam the sea bass fillets for 5–7 minutes until just cooked through.

- Add the fresh coriander leaves to the prepared dressing and mix well. Transfer the steamed sea bass fillets to a serving plate and top generously with the prepared dressing. Serve with Jasmine Rice (pages 142 and 144).

NOODLE AND
RICE DISHES

When it comes to noodles, Thailand's most famous dish is undoubtedly pad thai – literally, 'Thai stir-fry'. This rice noodle stir-fry is made sweet and slightly sour with fish sauce and tamarind paste, and is as delicious as its fame and reputation suggest.

Wide, flat rice noodles are used to make pad see ew (stir-fried noodles with soy sauce). Stir-fried in soy sauce, the noodles are allowed to catch in the pan to add a smoky flavour to the dish. Stir-fried noodles are an abundantly available Thai street-food dish, and are a convenient and quick one-pan meal to prepare at home for lunch.

Thai jasmine rice is soft and fragrant, perfect for soaking up stir-fry and curry sauces, while sticky rice is the perfect accompaniment to grilled meats and dipping sauces.

THAI FRIED NOODLES – PAD THAI

Serves 1–2

100g dry thin rice noodle sticks
2 tablespoons Tamarind Paste (page 188)
1 tablespoon fish sauce
Pinch of white pepper
1 tablespoon palm sugar
1 tablespoon water
1 tablespoon vegetable oil
2 shallots, finely chopped
1 garlic clove, finely chopped
30g firm tofu, chopped
125g raw king prawns
1 egg
Small handful fresh beansprouts
Small handful chopped roasted peanuts (page 177)
2–3 fresh lime wedges

- Put the dry rice noodles in a large bowl and cover with boiling water. Soak for 20 minutes, or according to the packet instructions, mixing a few times until the noodles are separated. Drain and rinse briefly with cold water. Drain once more and set aside.

- Put the tamarind paste, fish sauce, white pepper, sugar and water in a small bowl. Mix well and set aside.

- Heat a wok or large frying pan over a medium-high heat. When the pan is hot, add the oil, shallots, garlic and tofu and stir-fry for 20–30 seconds. Add the king prawns and stir-fry for 1 minute.

- Add the soaked noodles and the prepared sauce. Stir-fry for 1 minute.

- Push the ingredients in the pan to one side with a spatula. Crack the egg into the pan, allow to set for 10–15 seconds and then use the spatula to break the egg up. As it just begins to set, stir well to combine with the other ingredients.

- Add the beansprouts and chopped roasted peanuts and stir-fry for 1 minute. Transfer the Thai fried noodles to a serving plate and serve with lime wedges.

STIR-FRIED NOODLES WITH SOY
SAUCE – PAD SEE EW

Serves 1–2

100g dry wide rice noodle sticks (10mm)
1 tablespoon oyster sauce
1 teaspoon thin soy sauce
1 teaspoon thick soy sauce
2 teaspoons sweet soy sauce
1 teaspoon fish sauce
Pinch of white pepper
½ teaspoon sugar
1 tablespoon water
1 tablespoon vegetable oil
2 shallots, finely chopped
1 garlic clove, finely chopped
125g skinless, boneless chicken thigh, thinly sliced
1 egg
1–2 pak choi leaves, roughly chopped
Small handful fried or toasted cashew nuts (page 176)

- Put the dry rice noodles in a large bowl and cover with boiling water. Soak for 20 minutes, or according to the packet instructions, mixing a few times until the noodles are separated. Drain and rinse briefly with cold water. Drain once more and set aside.

- Put the oyster sauce, thin soy sauce, thick soy sauce, sweet soy sauce, fish sauce, white pepper, sugar and water in a small bowl. Mix well and set aside.

- Heat a wok or large frying pan over a medium-high heat. When the pan is hot, add the oil, shallots and garlic and stir-fry for 20–30 seconds. Add the sliced chicken and stir-fry for 2 minutes until the chicken is golden.

- Push the ingredients in the pan to one side with a spatula. Crack the egg into the pan, allow to set for 10–15 seconds and then use the spatula to break the egg up. As it just begins to set, stir well to combine with the other ingredients.

- Add the soaked noodles and the prepared sauce. Stir-fry for 2–3 minutes, allowing the noodles and egg to catch in the pan for 20–30 seconds at a time until well charred.

- Add the pak choi and cashew nuts and mix well. Stir-fry for a few more seconds, transfer the stir-fried noodles to a serving plate, dress with a touch more sweet soy sauce if desired and serve with Fish Sauce and Chillies (page 168) on the side.

BEEF NOODLES – PAD SEE EW

With a good heat in your wok or frying pan, the delicious smoky flavour and char takes this simple noodle dish to a higher level.

Serves 1–2

1 tablespoon oyster sauce
1 teaspoon thin soy sauce
1 teaspoon thick soy sauce
1 teaspoon sweet soy sauce
1 teaspoon fish sauce
Pinch of white pepper
½ teaspoon sugar
1 tablespoon water
100g dry wide rice noodle sticks (10mm)
1 tablespoon vegetable oil
2 shallots, finely chopped
1 garlic clove, finely chopped
125–150g Marinated Stir-Fry Beef (page 61)
1 egg
1–2 pak choi leaves, roughly chopped
Small handful toasted or fried cashew nuts (page 176)

- Put the oyster sauce, thin soy sauce, thick soy sauce, sweet soy sauce, fish sauce, white pepper, sugar and water in a small bowl. Mix well and set aside.

- Put the dry rice noodles in a large bowl and cover with boiling water. Soak for 20 minutes, mixing a few times until the noodles are separated. Drain and rinse briefly with cold water. Drain once more and set aside.

- Heat a wok or large frying pan over a medium-high heat. When the pan is hot, add the oil, shallots and garlic and stir-fry for 20–30 seconds. Add the marinated steak and stir-fry for 1 minute until the steak is evenly browned.

- Push the ingredients in the pan to one side with a spatula. Crack the egg into the pan, allow to set for 10–15 seconds and then use the spatula to break the egg up. As it just begins to set, stir well to combine with the other ingredients.

- Add the soaked noodles and the prepared sauce. Stir-fry for 2–3 minutes, allowing the noodles and egg to catch in the pan for 20–30 seconds at a time until well charred.

- Add the pak choi leaves and cashew nuts and mix well. Stir-fry for a few more seconds, transfer the beef noodles to a serving plate and serve with Fish Sauce and Chillies (page 168) on the side.

DRUNKEN NOODLES – PAD KEE MAO

Serves 1–2

1 tablespoon oyster sauce
1 teaspoon thin soy sauce
½ teaspoon thick soy sauce
1 teaspoon sweet soy sauce
1 teaspoon fish sauce
Pinch of white pepper
½ teaspoon sugar
1 tablespoon water
100g dry rice noodle sticks (I use 10mm sticks)
1 tablespoon vegetable oil
2 shallots, sliced
2 garlic cloves, finely chopped
1 red bird's-eye chilli, thinly sliced
1 mild red chilli pepper or ¼ red bell pepper, finely
  chopped
125g skinless, boneless chicken thigh, thinly sliced
1 carrot, thinly sliced
1 egg
1–2 pak choi or cabbage leaves, roughly chopped
1 spring onion, thinly sliced
1 handful fresh basil leaves (see note on page 13)

- Put the oyster sauce, thin soy sauce, thick soy sauce, sweet soy sauce, fish sauce, white pepper, sugar and water in a small bowl. Mix well and set aside.

- Put the dry rice noodles in a large bowl and cover with boiling water. Soak for 20 minutes, mixing a few times until the noodles are separated. Drain and rinse briefly with cold water. Drain once more and set aside.

- Heat a wok or large frying pan over a medium-high heat. When the pan is hot, add the oil, shallots, garlic and red chillies/red pepper. Stir-fry for 20–30 seconds. Add the sliced chicken and carrot and stir-fry for 2 minutes until the chicken is golden.

- Push the ingredients in the pan to one side with a spatula. Crack the egg into the pan, allow to set for 10–15 seconds and then use the spatula to break the egg up. As it just begins to set, stir well to combine with the other ingredients.

- Add the soaked noodles and the prepared sauce. Stir-fry for 2–3 minutes, allowing the noodles and egg to catch in the pan for 20–30 seconds at a time until well charred.

- Add the pak choi leaves, sliced spring onion and basil leaves. Mix well and cook for just a few more seconds. Transfer to a serving plate and serve with Fish Sauce and Chillies (page 168) on the side.

STIR-FRIED NOODLES

Serves 1–2

1 tablespoon oyster sauce
1 teaspoon thin soy sauce
1 teaspoon fish sauce
Pinch of white pepper
½ teaspoon palm sugar
50ml light stock or water
1 x nest thin wheat noodles
1 tablespoon vegetable oil
1 shallot, thinly sliced
1 garlic clove, finely chopped
2 small button mushrooms, halved and sliced
Small handful fresh beansprouts
1 spring onion, sliced
Small handful fresh coriander leaves, roughly chopped

- Put the oyster sauce, thin soy sauce, fish sauce, white pepper, sugar and light stock or water in a bowl. Mix well and set aside.

- Put the dried noodle nest in a heatproof bowl and cover with boiling water. Let the noodles soak for about 3 minutes, stirring once or twice to separate them as they soak. Drain and rinse the noodles in cold water to stop them becoming too soft, drain well once again and set aside.

- Heat a wok or large frying pan over a medium heat. Add the oil, shallot, garlic and mushrooms. Stir- fry for 1 minute.

- Add the beansprouts and the prepared sauce. Stir-fry for 1–2 minutes, or until the sauce is absorbed and the noodles and beansprouts are sizzling hot. Add the spring onion, mix once more and transfer to a serving plate. Garnish with fresh coriander leaves and serve.

JASMINE RICE (RICE COOKER METHOD)

Serves 1–2 (makes around 300g cooked rice)

1 rice cooker cup of jasmine rice

- Put the jasmine rice in a bowl and cover with fresh water. Mix the rice briefly by hand to agitate it – the water will become cloudy as excess starch is released from the rice. Drain the water and repeat the process until the water is clear. Give the rice a final rinse with water, drain well and tip into the rice cooker pot.

- Add water to the '1 cup' level indicated in your rice cooker and cook on 'long grain' setting. When the rice is cooked, fluff it up with a rice spoon, close the lid and leave on the 'keep warm' setting for 10 minutes. The rice is now ready to serve.

For fried rice:

- Remove the rice from the pot and spread it out on a large plate. Set aside for 5 minutes. After 5 minutes, transfer the rice to a different plate, flipping the rice over as you do so (you'll see excess moisture left behind on the first plate). Fan the rice with the lid of a food container for 3–4 minutes until it has completely cooled down. Transfer the cooked and cooled rice to a lidded container and chill in the fridge overnight before using in your favourite fried rice dishes.

To serve:

- Spoon the rice into one or two serving bowls. Tip each rice bowl upside down on to a serving plate and lift the bowl to reveal the shaped rice dome. Serve with your favourite soup and stir-fry dishes.

JASMINE RICE (STOVETOP METHOD)

Serves 1–2

150g jasmine rice
225ml cold water

- Put the jasmine rice in a bowl and cover with fresh water. Mix the rice briefly by hand to agitate it – the water will become cloudy as excess starch is released from the rice. Drain the water and repeat the process until the water is clear. Give the rice a final rinse with water, drain well and tip into a saucepan.

- Add the cold water. Bring to the boil over a high heat and, as soon as the water begins to boil, reduce the heat to the lowest available setting and cover the pan with a lid. Let the rice cook for 12 minutes. Remove from the heat and let the rice stand for another 10 minutes, resisting the urge to lift the lid. Fluff up the rice with a fork and it's ready to serve.

- Spoon the rice into one or two serving bowls. Tip each rice bowl upside down on to a serving plate and lift the bowl to reveal the shaped rice dome. Serve with your favourite soup and stir-fry dishes.

EGG FRIED RICE – KAO PAD KHAI

Serves 1–2

1 tablespoon vegetable oil
1 shallot, finely chopped
2 garlic cloves, finely chopped
1 egg
1 portion cooked and cooled jasmine rice (pages 142 and 144)
1 teaspoon thin soy sauce
Dash of thick soy sauce
1 teaspoon fish sauce
Pinch of white pepper
1 spring onion, thinly sliced
Small handful fresh coriander leaves, roughly chopped

• Heat a wok or large frying pan over a medium heat. Add the vegetable oil, shallot and garlic. Stir-fry for 20–30 seconds until aromatic. Add the egg and cook for 20–30 seconds, breaking the egg up as it sets in the pan. Add the cooked rice, mix well and stir-fry for 2–3 minutes, or until piping hot. Add the thin soy sauce, thick soy sauce and fish sauce and mix well.

- Increase the heat to high and continue to stir-fry the rice for a further minute or so until the texture is dry and the rice grains appear to pop or dance around the middle of the wok. Add the white pepper, spring onion and fresh coriander, mix well once more and serve.

COCONUT RICE (RICE COOKER METHOD)

Serves 1–2

> 1 rice cooker cup of jasmine rice
> 150ml coconut milk

- Put the jasmine rice in a bowl and cover with fresh water. Mix the rice briefly by hand to agitate it – the water will become cloudy as excess starch is released from the rice. Drain the water and repeat the process until the water is clear. Give the rice a final rinse with water, drain well and tip into the rice cooker pot.

- Add the coconut milk to the rice and mix briefly. Add water until the liquid reaches the '1 cup' level indicated in your rice cooker, mix briefly once more and cook on 'long grain' setting. When the rice is cooked, fluff it up with a rice spoon, close the lid and leave on the 'keep warm' setting for 10 minutes. The rice is now ready to serve.

For fried rice:

- Remove the rice from the pot and spread it out on a large plate. Set aside for 5 minutes. After 5 minutes, transfer the rice to a different plate, flipping the rice over as you do so (you'll see excess moisture left behind on the first plate). Fan the rice with the lid of a food container for 3–4 minutes until it has completely cooled down. Transfer the cooked and cooled rice to a lidded container and chill in the fridge overnight before using in your favourite fried rice dishes.

To serve:

- Spoon the rice into one or two serving bowls. Tip each rice bowl upside down on to a serving plate and lift the bowl to reveal the shaped rice dome. Serve with your favourite soup and stir-fry dishes.

COCONUT RICE (STOVETOP METHOD)

Serves 1–2

160g jasmine rice
150ml coconut milk
75ml water

- Put the jasmine rice in a bowl and cover with fresh water. Mix the rice briefly by hand to agitate it – the water will become cloudy as excess starch is released from the rice. Drain the water and repeat the process until the water is clear. Give the rice a final rinse with water, drain well and tip into a saucepan.

- Add the coconut milk and cold water and mix briefly. Bring to the boil over a high heat and, as soon as the water begins to boil, reduce the heat to the lowest available setting and cover the pan with a lid. Let the rice cook for 12 minutes. Remove from the heat and let the rice stand for another 10 minutes, resisting the urge to lift the lid. Fluff up the rice with a fork and it's ready to serve.

- Spoon the rice into one or two serving bowls. Tip each rice bowl upside down on to a serving plate and lift the bowl to reveal the shaped rice dome. Serve with your favourite soup and stir-fry dishes.

STICKY RICE (RICE COOKER METHOD)

Cooking sticky rice the traditional way requires a little forward planning, as the rice needs to soak overnight before being steamed. My rice cooker delivers acceptable results without such preparation, which is just one more reason why I love it so much and would highly recommend that you get one.

Serves 1–2

1 rice cooker cup (approx. 150g) Thai glutinous rice

- Put the glutinous rice in a bowl and cover with fresh water. Mix the rice briefly by hand to agitate it – the water will become cloudy as excess starch is released from the rice. Drain the water and repeat the process until the water is clear. Give the rice a final rinse with water, drain well and tip into the rice cooker pot.

- Add water to the '1.5' cup level indicated in your rice cooker and cook on 'short grain' setting. When the rice is cooked, spoon on to one or two serving plates.

- Serve with Pork Salad (page 112), Grilled Chicken (page 50) or Northern Thai-Style Sausage Meatballs (page 41).

STICKY RICE (STEAMER METHOD)

Serves 1–2

1 cup (approx. 150g) Thai glutinous rice

- Put the glutinous rice in a bowl and cover with fresh water. Mix the rice briefly by hand to agitate it – the water will become cloudy as excess starch is released from the rice. Drain the water and repeat the process until the water is clear. Cover with fresh water once more and set aside in the fridge overnight. Drain the rice well once more before use.

- Prepare a steamer with boiling water and reduce the heat to a simmer. Line a steamer basket with a muslin or cheese-cloth and spread the drained rice over the surface. Steam the rice for about 25 minutes, or until it reaches your preferred consistency.

- Serve with Pork Salad (page 112), Grilled Chicken (page 50) or Northern Thai-Style Sausage Meatballs (page 41).

CHICKEN OVER RICE – KHAO MAN GAI

Serves 1–2

450ml light stock or water
¼ teaspoon sea salt
225g skinless, boneless chicken thighs
1 rice cooker cup of jasmine rice
1 garlic clove, crushed
Small piece of ginger (about the size of 1 garlic clove)
Pinch of white pepper
Small handful fresh coriander leaves, finely chopped
7 fresh cucumber slices, to serve

- Put the light stock or water and sea salt in a saucepan. Bring to the boil, add the chicken thighs, reduce the heat to low and simmer for 25 minutes. Remove the chicken thighs from the stock and set aside.

- Put the jasmine rice in a bowl and cover with fresh water. Mix the rice briefly by hand to agitate it – the water will become cloudy as excess starch is released from the rice. Drain the water and repeat the process until the water is clear. Give the rice a final rinse with water, drain well and tip into a saucepan.

- *In a rice cooker:* Put the rice into the inner bowl of a rice cooker and add the stock used to cook the chicken to the level 1 mark. Add the garlic and ginger. Cook on the 'long grain' setting of your rice cooker for around 20 minutes. When the rice is cooked, stir with a rice spoon to fluff up the grains and leave on 'keep warm' mode for 10 minutes.

- *In a saucepan on the stovetop:* Put the rice into the saucepan. Add 225ml of the stock used to cook the chicken. Add the garlic and ginger. Bring to the boil over a high heat and, as soon as the water begins to boil reduce the heat to the lowest available setting and cover the pan with a lid. Let the rice cook for 12 minutes. Remove from the heat and let the rice stand for another 10 minutes, resisting the urge to lift the lid. Fluff up the rice with a fork and it's ready to serve.

- Bring the remaining stock to the boil, lower the heat and simmer for 1 minute. Add the white pepper and mix well. Pour the soup into a serving bowl.

- Arrange the cooked rice on a serving plate. Slice the cooked chicken thighs and place on top of the rice. Garnish with fresh coriander, and serve with the soup, Fermented Soybean Dipping Sauce (page 166) and fresh cucumber slices.

PRAWN PINEAPPLE FRIED RICE
– KHAO PAD SAPPAROD

Serves 1–2

1 fresh pineapple, or pineapple pieces from a tin (about
    80g drained weight)

1 tablespoon vegetable oil

80g raw king prawns

1 shallot, finely chopped

1 egg

1 portion cooked and cooled Jasmine Rice (pages 142 and
    144)

1 teaspoon curry powder

Pinch of turmeric

Pinch of sea salt

Pinch of sugar

1 teaspoon thin soy sauce

Dash of fish sauce

Pinch of white pepper

Small handful cashew nuts (about 25g)

Small handful raisins (about 15g)

Small handful fresh coriander leaves and stems, finely
    chopped

1 heaped teaspoon Crispy Fried Shallots (page 174)

- If using a fresh pineapple, cut the fruit lengthwise. Score the inside of the pineapple, remove the core and cut the fruit into small bite-sized pieces. If you'd like to serve the fried rice inside the pineapple, scrape out any remaining pineapple flesh and pat the inside of the pineapple dry with kitchen paper.

- Heat a wok or large frying pan over a medium-high heat. Add the vegetable oil and king prawns and stir-fry for around 2 minutes, until the prawns are beginning to turn pink and are almost cooked. Remove the prawns from the pan and set aside. Add a touch more oil to the pan if necessary. Add the shallot and stir-fry for 30–40 seconds.

- Push the ingredients in the pan to one side with a spatula. Crack the egg into the pan, allow to set for 10–15 seconds and then use the spatula to break the egg up. As it just begins to set, stir well to combine with the other ingredients.

- Add the jasmine rice and press on it with a ladle to break up any clumps (a potato masher also works well for this). Stir-fry for 1 minute. Add the curry powder, turmeric, sea salt, sugar, thin soy sauce and fish sauce. Stir-fry for another 1 minute.

- Add the white pepper, cashew nuts, raisins and pineapple pieces. Stir-fry for 30–40 seconds. Pour the fried rice into the pineapple shell or on to a serving plate, garnish with fresh coriander and crispy fried shallots and serve.

CHILLI AND BASIL FRIED RICE
– KHAO PAD KAPHRAO

Serves 1–2

2 teaspoons oyster sauce

1 teaspoon thin soy sauce

½ teaspoon thick soy sauce

1 teaspoon fish sauce

½ teaspoon caster sugar

1 shallot, finely chopped

2 garlic cloves, finely chopped

2–3 red bird's-eye chillies, thinly sliced

1 tablespoon vegetable oil

1 portion cooked and cooled Jasmine Rice (pages 142 and 144)

Handful fresh basil leaves (see note on page 13)

- Put the oyster sauce, thin soy sauce, thick soy sauce, fish sauce and caster sugar in a bowl. Mix well and set aside.

- Put the shallot, garlic and red chillies in a pestle and mortar. Pound to a fine paste. Transfer the paste to a small bowl and set aside.

- Heat a wok or large frying pan over a medium-high heat. Add the vegetable oil and the prepared paste and stir-fry for 20–30 seconds until aromatic. Add the jasmine rice and press on it with a ladle to break up any clumps (a potato masher also works well for this). Stir-fry for 1 minute.

- Add the prepared sauce and stir-fry for 1–2 minutes until the sauce has been absorbed by the rice. Switch off the heat, add the fresh basil leaves and mix once more.

- Pour the chilli and basil fried rice on to a serving plate. Top with a Crispy Fried Egg (page 192) and serve with Fish Sauce and Chillies (page 168).

TOM YUM STYLE FRIED RICE WITH PORK

Serves 1–2

1 tablespoon Chilli Paste (page 163)

1 teaspoon oyster sauce

1 teaspoon thin soy sauce

Dash of fish sauce

½ teaspoon caster sugar

50ml light chicken stock

1 shallot, finely chopped

2 garlic cloves, finely chopped

½ inch (1.3cm) piece of galangal, finely chopped (about
the size of 1 garlic clove)

1 red bird's-eye chilli, thinly sliced

1 generous teaspoon lemongrass (white part only), thinly
sliced

1 makrut lime leaf, thinly sliced

1 tablespoon vegetable oil

100g pork mince

2 small white button mushrooms, roughly chopped

3 cherry tomatoes, halved

1 egg

1 portion cooked and cooled Jasmine Rice (pages 142 and
144)

1 spring onion, thinly sliced

- Put the chilli paste, oyster sauce, thin soy sauce, fish sauce, caster sugar and light chicken stock in a bowl and mix well.

- Put the shallot, garlic, galangal, red chilli, lemongrass and lime leaf in a pestle and mortar. Pound to a fine paste. Transfer the paste to a small bowl and set aside.

- Heat a wok or large frying pan over a medium-high heat. Add the vegetable oil and the prepared paste and stir-fry for 20 seconds. Add the pork mince and stir-fry for around 1 minute, until the pork is beginning to brown. Add the mushrooms and cherry tomatoes and stir-fry for a further 30–40 seconds.

- Push the ingredients in the pan to one side with a spatula. Crack the egg into the pan, allow to set for 10–15 seconds and then use the spatula to break the egg up. As it just begins to set, stir well to combine with the other ingredients.

- Add the prepared sauce, mix well and stir-fry for 1 minute until the sauce reduces slightly. Add the jasmine rice and press on it with a ladle to break up any clumps (a potato masher also works well for this). Stir-fry for 1–2 minutes until piping hot.

- Pour the tom yum style fried rice with pork on to a serving plate, garnish with spring onion and fresh coriander and serve.

DIPS, SAUCES, CURRY PASTES AND EXTRAS

One of the real delights of ordering a takeaway meal is surely being free to choose from such a wide array of flavours, condiments and dishes – variety is the spice of life, after all. While coming under the 'fast food' umbrella, your takeaway chef works hard before service to create all manner of curry pastes, dipping sauces and garnishes, each one designed to ensure that your chosen meal arrives looking and tasting delicious.

This chapter includes recipes for a selection of essential components that you can use from beginning to end to build your perfect Thai takeaway style meal.

PEANUT DIPPING SAUCE – NAM JIM SATAY

Makes approx. 125ml

100ml coconut milk
1½ teaspoons Red Curry Paste (page 179, or from a tub)
2 teaspoons fish sauce
1 teaspoon thin soy sauce
1 teaspoon Tamarind Paste (page 188)
1 generous teaspoon palm sugar or brown sugar
4 tablespoons unsalted roasted peanuts (page 177),
  ground or pounded in a pestle and mortar (about 20g)
50ml water

- Heat a wok or saucepan over a medium heat. Add the coconut milk, bring to the boil and add the red curry paste. Reduce the heat to low and stir-fry the curry paste and coconut milk together for 1–2 minutes until aromatic.

- Add the fish sauce, thin soy sauce, tamarind paste and sugar. Mix well.

- Add the roasted peanuts and water and mix well. Simmer for 2–3 minutes until the sauce reaches your desired consistency.

- Pour the peanut sauce into a dipping bowl and serve with Chicken Satay (page 48).

CHILLI PASTE – NAM PRIK PAO

This fragrant, spicy chilli paste is great served alongside a Thai-style Omelette (page 120), or it can be used to make Cashew Chicken Stir-Fry (page 70).

Makes approx. 100g

3 tablespoons vegetable oil
4 shallots, finely chopped
4 garlic cloves, finely chopped
1½ tablespoons palm sugar or light brown sugar
1 tablespoon water
½ teaspoon thin soy sauce
1 tablespoon fish sauce
½ teaspoon Tamarind Paste (page 188)
¼ teaspoon shrimp paste (optional)
2 tablespoons Roasted Chilli Flakes (page 171)

• Heat a wok or frying pan over a medium heat. Add the oil and shallots and stir-fry for 3–4 minutes. Add the garlic and stir-fry for another 3–4 minutes until the ingredients are golden and aromatic.

- Add the sugar, water, thin soy sauce, fish sauce and tamarind paste. Add the shrimp paste if desired. Mix well. Add the chilli flakes and stir-fry for 2–3 minutes until the chilli paste is slightly thick. Transfer to a bowl and set aside to cool completely. Cover and store in the fridge until needed. The chilli paste will keep well in the fridge for 3 days.

SPICY DIPPING SAUCE – NAM JIM JAEW

Gochugaru (Korean chilli flakes) work well in this recipe if
you don't have Thai-style roasted chilli flakes.

Serves 1–2

1 shallot, finely chopped
1 teaspoon Roasted Chilli Flakes (page 171), or 1
    teaspoon gochugaru
1 spring onion, thinly sliced
Small handful fresh coriander leaves, finely chopped
1 tablespoon Toasted Rice (page 178)
2 tablespoons fish sauce
2 tablespoons fresh lime juice
1 teaspoon palm sugar

- Put the shallot, roasted chilli flakes, spring onion, fresh
  coriander and half of the toasted rice in a bowl. Set aside.

- Put the fish sauce, lime juice and palm sugar in a separate
  small bowl. Mix well.

- Combine the prepared sauce with the other ingredients
  and mix thoroughly. Pour the dipping sauce into a serving
  bowl, garnish with the remaining toasted rice and serve
  with Grilled Chicken (page 50) or your favourite grilled
  meat or fish.

FERMENTED SOYBEAN DIPPING
SAUCE – NAM JIM TOW JEAW

Serves 1–2

1 garlic clove, finely chopped
1 small piece of ginger, grated (about the same size as
    1 garlic clove)
1 red bird's-eye chilli, thinly sliced
1 teaspoon fresh coriander stems, thinly sliced
1 heaped tablespoon fermented soybean paste (Healthy
    Boy is a good brand)
1 teaspoon thin soy sauce
1 teaspoon thick soy sauce
1 teaspoon white vinegar
1 teaspoon caster sugar

- Put the garlic, ginger, chilli and fresh coriander stems in a pestle and mortar. Pound to a rough paste. Transfer the paste to a small bowl and set aside.

- Put the fermented soybean paste, thin soy sauce, thick soy sauce, white vinegar and caster sugar in a small bowl. Mix briefly. Add the prepared paste and mix well once more.

- Transfer the fermented soybean dipping sauce to a dipping bowl and serve with Chicken Over Rice (page 152).

SEAFOOD DIPPING SAUCE – NAM JIM SEAFOOD

Serves 1–2

2 garlic cloves, finely chopped
1–2 green bird's-eye chillies, thinly sliced
1 teaspoon fresh coriander stems, thinly sliced
1 tablespoon fish sauce
1 tablespoon fresh lime juice
1 teaspoon caster sugar
Small handful fresh coriander leaves, roughly chopped

- Put the garlic, chillies and fresh coriander stems in a pestle and mortar. Pound to a rough paste. Transfer the paste to a small bowl and set aside.

- Put the fish sauce, lime juice and caster sugar in a small bowl. Mix briefly. Add the prepared paste and mix well once more. Transfer the seafood dipping sauce to a dipping bowl, garnish with fresh coriander leaves and serve with seafood or Fresh Spring Rolls (page 23).

FISH SAUCE AND CHILLIES – NAM PRIK PLA

Serves 1–2

3 tablespoons fish sauce
1 tablespoon fresh lime juice, or to taste
2 red bird's-eye chillies, thinly sliced
2 garlic cloves, thinly sliced
1 teaspoon palm sugar or light brown sugar

- Put the fish sauce, lime juice, chillies, garlic and sugar in a bowl. Mix well.

- Serve as a condiment as desired. It's particularly good on top of a Crispy Fried Egg (page 192) with a plate of Pork and Holy Basil Stir-Fry (page 80). The sauce will keep well in a covered bowl in the fridge for up to 3 days.

SWEET CHILLI SAUCE – NAM JIM GAI

Serves 1–2

2 tablespoons fish sauce
100ml rice wine vinegar
150g caster sugar
3 teaspoons dried chilli flakes
50ml water
1 tablespoon potato starch mixed with 2 tablespoons cold
    water

- Put the fish sauce, rice wine vinegar, sugar, chilli flakes and water in a saucepan and mix well.

- Bring to the boil over a medium-high heat, reduce the heat to low and simmer for 8–10 minutes, or until the sauce is slightly reduced. Increase the heat to medium and gradually add the starch and water mix to the simmering sauce, stirring well until the sauce reaches the desired consistency – it should be slightly thick, and will thicken more as it cools (you may not need all the mix).

- Set the sauce aside to cool completely. The sweet chilli sauce will keep well in the fridge for up to 1 month.

CUCUMBER RELISH – AJAD

Serves 1–2

2 tablespoons white vinegar
2 tablespoons water
1 teaspoon sugar, or to taste
Pinch of sea salt
¼ cucumber, roughly chopped
3 shallots, roughly chopped
1 red bird's-eye chilli, thinly sliced (optional)

- Put the white vinegar, water, sugar and sea salt in a small saucepan. Warm over a medium heat for 1 minute, stirring well until the sugar is dissolved. Switch off the heat.

- Add the cucumber, shallots and red chilli. Mix well once more and set aside to cool completely.

- Pour the cucumber relish into a serving bowl and serve alongside Fish Cakes (page 56) or Chicken Satay (page 48). The relish will keep well in a covered bowl in the fridge for up to 3 days.

ROASTED CHILLI FLAKES – PRIK BON

Typically offered as a condiment to be added to a variety of dishes including noodles, soups and salads, you can make these chilli flakes as hot or as mild as you like by adjusting the quantity of large or small dried chillies (larger dried chillies are typically mild and small dried chillies are typically hot and spicy).

12 large dried red chillies
3 small dried red chillies

- Heat a dry wok or large frying pan over a medium heat. Add the dried chillies and dry-fry for 5–6 minutes, or until the chillies have darkened in colour a little. Set aside to cool completely.

- Transfer the chillies to a spice grinder, coffee grinder or blender and pulse a few times until the mix reaches your preferred consistency. Transfer to a food-safe container, cover with a lid and set aside for use as needed. The roasted chilli flakes will keep well at room temperature for up to 1 month.

CRISPY FRIED GARLIC – KRATIEM JIAW

While you can purchase crispy fried garlic easily in supermarkets, it's worth making your own as you're rewarded with a delicious garlic oil by-product. Both the crispy garlic and the garlic-infused oil are delicious added to soups and stir-fry dishes.

Serves 4 (makes about 50g of crispy garlic)

12 garlic cloves
75ml vegetable oil

- Peel and finely chop the garlic cloves. Put the oil in a frying pan, add the chopped garlic and mix well.

- Place the pan over a medium-low heat. After a few minutes, the garlic will begin to sizzle in the oil. Stir regularly and fry the garlic for about 5 minutes, or until golden. Keep your attention on the garlic as it fries, and switch off the heat just before you think it's ready – the garlic will continue to colour in the oil.

- Strain the fried garlic from the oil using a fine-mesh sieve and set both the garlic and the frying oil aside to cool completely. Transfer the crispy fried garlic and garlic oil to separate food-safe containers, cover with lids and set aside for use as desired.

- The crispy garlic will keep well at room temperature for up to 3 days, and the garlic-infused oil will keep well in the fridge for up to 1 week.

CRISPY FRIED SHALLOTS – HOM JIAW

As a general rule, I fry one thinly sliced shallot per dish that I want to garnish, plus one more for snacking, because who can resist crispy fried shallots?

Serves 4 (makes about 50g of crispy shallots)

9 shallots
75ml vegetable oil

- Peel and finely chop the shallots. Put the oil in a frying pan, add the chopped shallots and mix well.

- Place the pan over a medium-low heat. After a few minutes, the shallots will begin to sizzle in the oil. Stir regularly and fry the shallots for about 7–8 minutes, or until golden. Keep your attention on the shallots as they fry, and switch off the heat just before you think they are ready – the shallots will continue to colour in the oil.

- Strain the fried shallots from the oil using a fine-mesh sieve and set both the shallots and the frying oil aside to cool completely. Transfer the crispy fried shallots and shallot oil to separate food-safe containers, cover with lids and set aside for use as desired.

- The crispy shallots will keep well at room temperature for up to 3 days, and the shallot-infused oil will keep well in the fridge for up to 1 week.

FRIED CASHEW NUTS

Vegetable oil for deep-frying
Handful cashew nuts (or as much as you need)

- Heat the oil for deep-frying to 180°C/350°F. Carefully drop the cashew nuts into the oil and fry for about 1 minute, or until golden brown. Remove from the oil with a slotted spoon, drain off any excess oil and set aside.

- Alternatively, heat a dry wok or large frying pan over a medium heat and dry-fry the cashew nuts for 2–3 minutes, stirring occasionally until the cashews are golden brown. Transfer to a plate and set aside to cool.

- Use as needed in your favourite stir-fry dishes.

DRY ROASTED PEANUTS

1 tablespoon raw peanuts

- Heat a dry wok or frying pan over a medium heat. Add the raw peanuts and dry-fry for 3–4 minutes, or until golden. Transfer to a bowl and set aside to cool.

- Use as needed in stir-fry dishes or salads.

TOASTED RICE – KHAO KHUA

This crispy toasted rice adds a crunchy texture to Pork Salad (page 112) and Spicy Dipping Sauce (page 165).

Serves 1–2

> 1 generous tablespoon glutinous rice or jasmine rice (or as much as you need)

- Heat a dry wok or large frying pan over a medium heat. Add the rice and toast in the pan for 8–10 minutes, or until most of the rice has turned golden in colour and the pleasant aroma of popcorn fills the air. Stir the rice occasionally as it toasts. Transfer the toasted rice to a pestle and mortar and set aside to cool briefly.

- Pound the rice to a coarse consistency and transfer to a small bowl. Use to make Pork Salad (page 112) or as desired.

- The toasted rice will keep well in a covered bowl at room temperature for up to 1 week.

RED CURRY PASTE – PRIK GAENG PED

Aromatic and spicy.

Makes about 125g

1½ teaspoons cumin seeds
1 tablespoon coriander seeds
1½ teaspoons white peppercorns
12 large dried red chillies (about 10g)
6 small dried red chillies (about 3g)
3 shallots, finely chopped
1 lemongrass stalk (white part only), finely chopped
Zest of 1 lime
6 garlic cloves, finely chopped
1 inch (2.5cm) piece galangal (about the size of 2 garlic
   cloves), finely chopped
1 tablespoon fresh coriander stems, thinly sliced
¼ teaspoon sea salt
1 teaspoon shrimp paste

- Heat a dry wok or frying pan over a medium heat. Add the cumin seeds, coriander seeds and white peppercorns and toast for 30–40 seconds until aromatic. Transfer to a pestle and mortar and set aside to cool briefly. Pound the spices to a coarse powder, transfer to a small bowl and set aside.

- Use scissors to cut the stems from the dried chillies. Cut each chilli down lengthwise and remove the seeds (use gloves if you're particularly sensitive to chillies). Cut the dried chillies into very small pieces, cover with boiling water and set aside until cool. Strain with a fine-mesh sieve and set the softened chilli pieces aside.

- Put the shallots, lemongrass, lime zest, garlic, galangal and fresh coriander stems in a pestle and mortar. Pound to a rough paste. Add the softened chillies and sea salt and continue pounding until all the ingredients are completely broken down. This will take some time and effort, and you should be careful to cover the pestle and mortar with the hand you're holding it steady with, to help block any rogue ingredients from splashing out towards your face. Don't look directly at the ingredients as you pound the paste.

- Carry on pounding until you're satisfied that there are no (or minimal) noticeable ingredients and the mix has become a smooth paste. Finally, add the shrimp paste and mix well. Transfer the curry paste to a bowl, cover and set aside until needed.

- Use as desired for red curry, or as an ingredient in Crispy Chicken Wings (page 46), Fish Cakes (page 56), Northern Thai-Style Sausage Meatballs (page 41) or Peanut Dipping Sauce (page 162).

- The paste will keep well in the fridge for up to 1 week, or in the freezer for up to 3 months.

MASSAMAN CURRY PASTE –
PRIK GAENG MASSAMAN

Massaman curry (page 86), or 'Muslim curry', is heavily influenced by Muslim traditions, with cinnamon and clove flavours cooked alongside beef or chicken as opposed to pork.

Makes about 125g

1½ teaspoons cumin seeds
1 tablespoon coriander seeds
½ teaspoon black peppercorns
12 large dried red chillies (about 10g)
3 small dried red chillies (about 1.5g)
3 shallots, finely chopped
1 lemongrass stalk (white part only), finely chopped
Zest of 1 lime
6 garlic cloves, finely chopped
1 inch (2.5cm) piece galangal (about the size of 2 garlic cloves), finely chopped
1 tablespoon fresh coriander stems, thinly sliced
¼ cinnamon stick
2 whole cloves
1 green cardamom pod, crushed
¼ teaspoon sea salt
1 teaspoon shrimp paste

- Heat a dry wok or frying pan over a medium heat. Add the cumin seeds, coriander seeds and black peppercorns and toast for 30–40 seconds until aromatic. Transfer to a pestle and mortar and set aside to cool briefly. Pound the spices to a coarse powder, transfer to a small bowl and set aside.

- Use scissors to cut the stems from the dried chillies. Cut each chilli down lengthwise and remove the seeds (use gloves if you're particularly sensitive to chillies). Cut the dried chillies into very small pieces, cover with boiling water and set aside until cool. Strain with a fine-mesh sieve and set the softened chilli pieces aside.

- Put the shallots, lemongrass, lime zest, garlic, galangal and fresh coriander stems in a pestle and mortar. Pound to a rough paste. Add the cinnamon stick, whole cloves and the seeds from the crushed cardamom pod. Add the softened chillies and sea salt and continue pounding until all of the ingredients are completely broken down. This will take some time and effort, and you should be careful to cover the pestle and mortar with the hand you're holding it steady with, to help block any rogue ingredients from splashing out towards your face. Don't look directly at the ingredients as you pound the paste.

- Carry on pounding until you're satisfied that there are no (or minimal) noticeable ingredients and the mix has become a smooth paste. Finally, add the shrimp paste and mix well. Transfer the curry paste to a bowl, cover and set aside until needed.

- Use to make Beef Massaman Curry (page 86).

- The paste will keep well in the fridge for up to 1 week, or in the freezer for up to 3 months.

PANANG CURRY PASTE – PRIK GAENG PANANG

Makes about 125g

1½ teaspoons cumin seeds
1 tablespoon coriander seeds
1½ teaspoons white peppercorns
12 large dried red chillies (about 10g)
6 small dried red chillies (about 3g)
3 shallots, finely chopped
1 lemongrass stalk (white part only), finely chopped
Zest of 1 lime
6 garlic cloves, finely chopped
1 inch (2.5cm) piece galangal (about the size of 2 garlic
    cloves), finely chopped
1 tablespoon fresh coriander stems, thinly sliced
2 tablespoons unsalted roasted peanuts (page 177)
¼ teaspoon sea salt
1 teaspoon shrimp paste

- Heat a dry wok or frying pan over a medium heat. Add the cumin seeds, coriander seeds and white peppercorns and toast for 30–40 seconds until aromatic. Transfer to a pestle and mortar and set aside to cool briefly. Pound the spices to a coarse powder, transfer to a small bowl and set aside.

- Use scissors to cut the stems from the dried chillies. Cut each chilli down lengthwise and remove the seeds (use gloves if you're particularly sensitive to chillies). Cut the dried chillies into very small pieces, cover with boiling water and set aside until cool. Strain with a fine-mesh sieve and set the softened chilli pieces aside.

- Put the shallots, lemongrass, lime zest, garlic, galangal and fresh coriander stems in a pestle and mortar. Pound to a rough paste. Add the softened chillies, roasted peanuts and sea salt and continue pounding until all of the ingredients are completely broken down. This will take some time and effort, and you should be careful to cover the pestle and mortar with the hand you're holding it steady with to help block any rogue ingredients from splashing out towards your face. Don't look directly at the ingredients as you pound the paste.

- Carry on pounding until you're satisfied that there are no (or minimal) noticeable ingredients and the mix has become a smooth paste. Finally, add the shrimp paste and mix well. Transfer the curry paste to a bowl, cover and set aside until needed.

- Use to make Panang Pork Curry (page 90).

- The paste will keep well in the fridge for up to 1 week, or in the freezer for up to 3 months.

THE THAI TAKEAWAY SECRET

GREEN CURRY PASTE – PRIK GAENG KHIAO WAAN

Makes about 125g

1½ teaspoons cumin seeds
1 tablespoon coriander seeds
½ teaspoon white peppercorns
6 green bird's-eye chillies, thinly sliced
1 mild green chilli, finely chopped
3 shallots, finely chopped
1 lemongrass stalk (white part only), finely chopped
Zest of 1 lime
6 garlic cloves, finely chopped
1 inch (2.5cm) piece galangal (about the size of 2 garlic cloves), finely chopped
1 tablespoon fresh coriander stems, thinly sliced
Small handful fresh basil leaves, finely chopped (see note on page 13)
¼ teaspoon sea salt
1 teaspoon shrimp paste

- Heat a dry wok or frying pan over a medium heat. Add the cumin seeds, coriander seeds and white peppercorns and toast for 30–40 seconds until aromatic. Transfer to a pestle and mortar and set aside to cool briefly. Pound the spices to a coarse powder, transfer to a small bowl and set aside.

186

- Put the green bird's-eye chillies, mild green chilli, shallots, lemongrass, lime zest, garlic, galangal, fresh coriander stems and basil leaves in a pestle and mortar. Pound to a rough paste. Add the sea salt and continue pounding until all of the ingredients are completely broken down. This will take some time and effort, and you should be careful to cover the pestle and mortar with the hand you're holding it steady with, to help block any rogue ingredients that might splash towards your face. Don't look directly at the ingredients as you pound the paste.

- Carry on pounding the curry paste until you're satisfied that there are no (or minimal) noticeable ingredients and the mix has become a smooth paste. Finally, add the shrimp paste and mix well. Transfer the curry paste to a bowl, cover and set aside until needed.

- Use to make Green Curry (page 88).

- The paste will keep well in the fridge for up to 1 week, or in the freezer for up to 3 months.

TAMARIND PASTE – MAKAAM PIAK

Tamarind blocks are widely available in supermarkets or online. They keep well for a good amount of time and can be used to make tamarind paste as and when you need it.

Makes about 3 tablespoons

25g dried tamarind block
50ml boiling water

- Put the dried tamarind block in a heatproof bowl. Cover with the boiling water, mix briefly and set aside for 30 minutes.

- Pour the tamarind and hot water through a sieve into a separate bowl. Press the tamarind block into the sieve to extract as much of the tamarind as possible, scraping the bottom of the sieve to collect the paste.

- Transfer the tamarind paste to a container, cover and set aside in the fridge and use as needed.

- The tamarind paste will keep well in the fridge for up to 3 days.

GARLIC IN OIL

When cooking dishes to order for busy takeaway shifts, many takeaways use rehydrated chopped garlic in oil (as opposed to fresh garlic), in stir-fry dishes and marinades. It's convenient and delicious, and although the flavour is different when compared to dishes cooked with fresh garlic, it's often preferred, particularly if you're used to your favourite dishes being cooked that way. Look for larger packs of dried chopped garlic in Chinese supermarkets, which are both superior to and less expensive than traditional supermarket brands.

Makes about 450g

100g dried chopped garlic
400ml boiling water
250ml vegetable oil
Pinch of sea salt

- Put the dried chopped garlic in a large heatproof bowl. Pour the boiling water over the chopped garlic, mix well and set aside for 5 minutes. Strain the garlic through a fine sieve.

- Put the garlic in a saucepan and cover with the vegetable oil. Place over a medium heat and let the mixture come to a sizzle, then reduce the heat to low and slowly fry the garlic for 10–12 minutes until aromatic. Add the sea salt and mix through. Set aside to cool completely, pour into a food-safe container with a tight-fitting lid and store in the fridge for up to 1 month.

LIGHT CHICKEN STOCK

Gentle in flavour and unseasoned, perfect for soups or stir-fry dishes.

Makes about 750ml

500g chicken wing tips
1 litre water
1 carrot
2 garlic cloves
½ teaspoon white peppercorns

- Put the wing tips in a large bowl. Cover with boiling water, mix once, drain and set aside.

- Transfer the chicken wing tips to a large saucepan. Add the litre of cold water, carrot, garlic and white peppercorns. Bring to the boil over a high heat. Once the mix is boiling, spoon off any foam in the water, reduce the heat to low and simmer for 3 hours.

- Strain the vegetables and peppercorns from the stock and return the stock to the heat. Bring back to the boil, reduce the heat to medium-low and simmer for 1 hour until the stock is reduced slightly. Set aside to cool completely. Transfer to a food-safe container and cover with a lid.

- The light stock will keep well in the fridge for up to 3 days or in the freezer for up to 3 months.

CRISPY FRIED EGG – KHAI DOW

If you've ever seen eggs cooked to accompany a traditional Scottish breakfast, you'll be very at home with Thai-style fried eggs. Cooked in generous amounts of oil, the edges of the egg turn deliciously crispy while the yolk remains just the right side of soft. Perfect served alongside a plate of warm rice.

Serves 1

50ml vegetable oil
1 egg

- Heat the oil in a wok or frying pan over a medium-high heat.

- Crack the egg into a small bowl then pour the egg into the hot oil. The white of the egg will bubble immediately.

- Use a spatula to spoon hot oil over the egg and fry for 30–40 seconds, until the edges of the egg white are golden brown and crispy and the yolk is still soft.

- Remove from the oil with a spatula, drain off any excess oil and serve.

DESSERTS AND DRINKS

While Thai meals don't typically include a sweet dessert course, some delicious sweet dishes can be enjoyed at any time and have become very well known, none more so than Coconut Sticky Rice with Mango (page 195). Sticky rice soaks up sweet and rich coconut milk and pairs perfectly with ripe fresh mango slices.

Many Thai dishes offer a powerful punch of chilli heat, so pairing them with drinks that will both soothe as well as satisfy is always a good idea. Ice-cold fruit- and coconut-based drinks can help to ensure you're ready to tackle another spoonful of your favourite hot dishes!

FRESH FRUIT SALAD – SOM TAM PHONLAMAI

Serves 4

1 red bird's-eye chilli
1 teaspoon dried shrimp
2 teaspoons palm sugar
6 cherry tomatoes, halved
2 teaspoons fish sauce
1 tablespoon fresh lime juice
1 handful fresh pineapple chunks (about 75g)
12 grapes
1 apple, peeled and cut into bite-sized pieces
2–3 fresh mint leaves

- Put the bird's-eye chilli in a pestle and mortar and pound well. Add the dried shrimp and palm sugar and pound a little more. Add the cherry tomatoes and pound once more just to bruise them a little. Add the fish sauce and fresh lime juice and mix well.

- Put the pineapple chunks, grapes and apple pieces in a large bowl. Add the pounded ingredients, mix well, garnish with a few fresh mint leaves if desired and serve.

COCONUT STICKY RICE WITH MANGO
– KHAO NIAO MAMUANG

This classic Thai dessert is best made with fresh diced mango, but the coconut rice is so delicious that it's also a treat with tinned mango chunks.

Serves 2–4

For the rice
    1 portion cooked sticky rice
    175ml coconut milk
    50g sugar
    Pinch of sea salt

For the dressing
    150ml coconut milk
    2 heaped teaspoons sugar
    Generous pinch of sea salt
    2 teaspoons rice flour, mixed with 2 tablespoons water

To serve
    2 fresh mangoes, peeled and diced or 300g tinned mango
        chunks (drained weight)
    1 teaspoon toasted sesame seeds (optional)

• Cook the sticky rice in a rice cooker (page 150) or steamer (page 151).

- When the rice is almost cooked, heat the coconut milk, sugar and sea salt over a medium-high heat. Bring to the boil, mix well until the sugar is dissolved, remove from the heat and set aside.

- Spoon the cooked sticky rice into a large bowl. Pour the prepared warm coconut milk mix over the rice and mix well with a rice spoon until fully combined. Cover the bowl and set aside for 30 minutes, or until completely cooled down.

- Just before serving make the dressing. Heat the coconut milk, sugar and sea salt over a medium-high heat. Bring to the boil, mix well until the sugar is dissolved, reduce the heat to low and simmer for 1–2 minutes until slightly reduced. Add the rice flour and water mix to the simmering coconut milk mix and stir through. Simmer and stir for a further minute until the sauce is slightly thickened.

- Ladle up portions of the sticky rice and fresh mango slices into serving bowls. Pour the warm sweet coconut milk mix over the rice, top with toasted sesame seeds if desired and serve.

- Keep leftover rice covered and refrigerate as soon as possible. To reheat, add 2–3 teaspoons of water to the rice and microwave for 45 seconds, or until piping hot. Mix well before serving.

BANANA IN COCONUT MILK – KLUAI BUAT CHI

Serves 1–2

175ml coconut milk
2 heaped teaspoons sugar
Generous pinch of sea salt
1 banana, sliced
2 teaspoons rice flour, mixed with 2 tablespoons water

- Put the coconut milk in a saucepan. Bring to the boil, add the sugar and sea salt and mix well until the sugar is dissolved.

- Reduce the heat to low, add the sliced banana and simmer for 2 minutes, stirring gently once or twice. Add the rice flour and water mix to the simmering coconut milk mix and stir through. Simmer and stir for a further minute until the sauce is slightly thickened.

- Pour the bananas in coconut milk into a serving bowl and serve.

CHOCOLATE AND BANANA PARATHA

Serves 1

1 frozen paratha bread (Shana brand is good)
1 heaped tablespoon chocolate spread
1 banana, sliced
1 tablespoon condensed milk

- Heat a dry frying pan over a medium heat. Add the frozen paratha and cook for 4 minutes, flipping the paratha and pressing down gently every 30 seconds. Set aside to cool briefly.

- Cut the paratha into small pieces and transfer to a serving bowl. Top with the chocolate spread, sliced bananas and condensed milk and serve.

COCONUT ICE CREAM

Serves 8

1 litre coconut milk
125g caster sugar
Pinch of sea salt
2 teaspoons vanilla extract

- Put the coconut milk in a saucepan. Bring to the boil, add the sugar and mix until dissolved. Remove from the heat, add the sea salt and mix once more. Set aside to cool completely.

- Add the vanilla extract and mix well once again.

- *In an ice cream maker:* Add the mix to the pre-frozen bowl of an ice cream maker and churn as per the instructions.

- *In a container:* Add the mix to a food-safe container with a lid and place in the freezer. Freeze for 6–8 hours. Remove the mix from the freezer every hour and whisk thoroughly. After 6 hours the coconut ice cream can be left in the freezer until needed.

- Serve the coconut ice cream with Fresh Fruit Salad (page 194) or Thai-Style Banana Fritters (page 200).

THAI-STYLE BANANA FRITTERS – KLUAY KAEK

Serves 1–2

60g rice flour
60g cornflour or custard powder
75g desiccated coconut
Pinch of sea salt
1 generous tablespoon caster sugar
½ teaspoon bicarbonate of soda
150–200ml water
Oil for deep-frying
1–2 bananas, each cut diagonally into 3 pieces
1 teaspoon toasted sesame seeds

- Put the rice flour, cornflour or custard powder, desiccated coconut, sea salt, sugar and bicarbonate of soda in a bowl. Slowly add the water, whisking thoroughly until the batter is smooth and slightly thick, with the consistency of double cream. You may not need all the water.

- Heat the oil for deep-frying to 180°C/350°F. In batches, dip banana pieces into the prepared batter and then drop carefully into the hot oil. Fry for about 4 minutes, or until crispy and golden. Repeat until all of the banana fritters are fried.

- Remove from the oil using a slotted spoon, drain off any excess oil and transfer to a serving bowl. Garnish with toasted sesame seeds and serve with Coconut Ice Cream (page 199).

MANGO SORBET

Serves 2

1 fresh ripe mango, peeled and diced, or 200g frozen
   mango chunks
5 tablespoons caster sugar
3 tablespoons coconut milk
50ml water
1 teaspoon fresh lime juice

- Put the mango, caster sugar, coconut milk, water and lime juice in a blender and blend until smooth. Pour the mango sorbet mix into a freezer-safe container, cover with a lid and freeze for 3 hours.

- Remove the sorbet from the freezer and use a fork to mix thoroughly. Return to the freezer for another 3 hours, mixing thoroughly again every hour during that time. Once you're happy with the consistency, the sorbet can be frozen completely.

- Use a fork to scrape and fluff up as much of the mango sorbet as you desire, transfer to a serving bowl and serve.

THAI ICED TEA – CHA YEN

Serves 1–2

> 2 teabags black tea, or 2 generous teaspoons black tea
> leaves
> 500ml boiling water
> 1 tablespoon caster sugar, or to taste
> 1 tablespoon evaporated milk
> 30ml condensed milk
> 7–8 ice cubes
> Dash of vanilla extract

- Make the tea as normal with the boiling water. When it is just brewed and piping hot, add the caster sugar, evaporated milk and condensed milk. Mix well. Set aside to cool to room temperature.

- Fill one or two serving cups with ice cubes and add the vanilla extract. Pour the tea over the ice into the serving cups. Stir well and serve.

FRUIT COOLER

Serves 1–2

150g frozen mango chunks
70g pineapple chunks (fresh or from a tin)
1 tablespoon caster sugar
Large handful ice cubes
1 fresh mint leaf

- Put the mango, pineapple and caster sugar in a blender. Blend until smooth. Add the ice cubes and blend once more until thick and pourable, adding a touch of water if a thinner consistency is desired.

- Pour the fruit cooler into a large glass, garnish with a fresh mint leaf if desired and serve.

ACKNOWLEDGEMENTS

Thanks to all my family and friends who have encouraged me in my food obsessions over the years, and to all at Little, Brown for doing the same. Thanks to Lynn Brown for her fabulous editing skills. Thanks to Rebecca for everything. Thanks to Louise Boyle for curry pastes and social anxiety understanding and experience, direct from Thailand! Thanks to Kirsty Bowker, Lisa, Karen Quinn and everyone online who gives me opinions, advice and inspiration. Thanks to all the restaurant, takeaway, fast food and street food workers who work so hard to create and serve delicious food.

Thanks to you if you're reading this book. I hope you'll try the recipes and, if you do, I hope you'll be very glad to have done so.

INDEX

bamboo shoots
  Chicken Crispy Spring Rolls
    43–5
  Chicken Jungle Curry 91–2
  Chicken Red Curry 84–5
  Green Curry 88–9
  Mixed Vegetables in Oyster
    Sauce 118–19
  Pork and Vegetable Spring
    Rolls 30–2
  Vegetable Spring Rolls 20–2
bananas
  Banana in Coconut Milk 197
  Chocolate and Banana
    Paratha 198
  Thai-style Banana Fritters
    200
basil 13
  Chilli and Basil Fried Rice
    156–7
  Pork and Holy Basil Stir-fry
    80–1
beansprouts
  Stir-fried Noodles 140–1
  Thai Fried Noodles 132–3

beef
  Beef Massaman Curry 86–7
  Beef Noodles 136–7
  Beef and Oyster Sauce Stir-
    fry 68–9
  Crying Tiger Steak 126–7
  Marinated Stir-fry Beef 61
bread
  Chicken and Prawn Toasts 54–5
  Chocolate and Banana
    Paratha 198

cabbage
  Drunken Noodles 138–9
  Instant Noodle Salad 114–15
  Mixed Salad with Peanut
    Dressing 106–7
  Vermicelli Bean Thread
    Noodle Stir-fry 66–7
carrots
  Beef Massaman Curry 86–7
  Cashew Chicken Stir-fry
    70–1
  Chicken Crispy Spring Rolls
    43–5

Chicken Jungle Curry 91–2
Drunken Noodles 138–9
Fresh Spring Rolls 23–4
Instant Noodle Salad 114–15
Light Chicken Stock 191
Mama's Crispy Volcano
    Chicken 2, 122–3
Mixed Salad with Peanut
    Dressing 106–7
Mixed Vegetables in Oyster
    Sauce 118–19
Mushroom Curry Puffs 26–7
Papaya Salad 110–11
Pork and Rice Soup 98–9
Pork and Vegetable Spring
    Rolls 30–2
Vegetable Spring Rolls 20–2
Vermicelli Bean Thread
    Noodle Stir-fry 66–7
cashew nuts
    Beef Massaman Curry 86–7
    Beef Noodles 136–7
    Cashew Chicken Stir-fry 70–1
    Fried Cashew Nuts 176
    Prawn Pineapple Fried Rice
        154–5
    Stir-fried Noodles with Soy
        Sauce 134–5
    Sweet and Sour Chicken Stir-
        fry 72–3
chicken
    Chicken Crispy Spring Rolls
        43–5
    Chicken and Ginger Stir-fry
        78–9
    Chicken Jungle Curry 2,
        91–2

Chicken Over Rice 152–3
Chicken Pineapple Stir-fry
    74–5
Chicken and Prawn Toasts
    54–5
Chicken Red Curry 84–5
Chicken Satay 48–9
Chicken Soup with Galangal
    102–3
Crispy Chicken for Stir-fry
    Dishes 65
Crispy Chicken Wings 46–7
Curry Chicken Noodle Soup
    104–5
Drunken Noodles 138–9
Glass Noodle Soup 96–7
Green Curry 88–9
Grilled Chicken 50–1
Grilled Chicken Salad 108–9
Light Chicken Stock 191
Mama's Crispy Volcano
    Chicken 2, 122–3
Marinated Stir-fry Chicken
    Breast 62
Marinated Stir-fry Chicken
    Thighs 63
Stir-fried Noodles with Soy
    Sauce 134–5
Sweet Chilli Chicken Balls
    52–3
Sweet and Sour Chicken Stir-
    fry 72–3
Thai Fried Chicken 124–5
chicken stock v, 191
Chilli Paste 163–4
    Cashew Chicken Stir-fry
        70–1

Prawn Hot and Sour Soup 100–1

Tom Yum Style Fried Rice with Pork 158–9

chillies 11, 13

Cashew Chicken Stir-fry 70–1

Chicken Jungle Curry 91–2

Chicken Soup with Galangal 102–3

Chilli and Basil Fried Rice 156–7

Chilli Paste 163–4

Cucumber Relish 170

Drunken Noodles 138–9

Fish Sauce and Chillies 168

Fresh Fruit Salad 194

Green Curry 88–9

Green Curry Paste 186–7

Instant Noodle Salad 114–15

Massaman Curry Paste 181–3

Panang Curry Paste 184–5

Panang Pork Curry 90

Papaya Salad 110–11

Pork and Holy Basil Stir-fry 80–1

Pork and Red Curry Stir-fry 82

Pork and Rice Soup 98–9

Pork Salad 112–13

Prawn Hot and Sour Soup 100–1

Red Curry Paste 179–80

Roasted Chilli Flakes 171

Seafood Dipping Sauce 167

Spicy Dipping Sauce 165

Steamed Sea Bass 130

Sweet Chilli Sauce 169

Tom Yum Style Fried Rice with Pork 158–9

see also sweet chilli sauce

Chocolate and Banana Paratha 198

coconut

Coconut Prawns 58

Thai-style Banana Fritters 200

coconut milk vi, 11

Banana in Coconut Milk 197

Beef Massaman Curry 86–7

Chicken Red Curry 84–5

Chicken Satay 48–9

Chicken Soup with Galangal 102–3

Coconut Ice Cream 199

Coconut Rice 147–9

Coconut Sticky Rice with Mango 195–6

Curry Chicken Noodle Soup 104–5

Green Curry 88–9

Mango Sorbet 201

Panang Pork Curry 90

Peanut Dipping Sauce 162

Pork Skewers 37–8

condensed milk

Chocolate and Banana Paratha 198

Thai Iced Tea 202

coriander 13

Corn Fritters 18–19

Crispy Chicken for Stir-fry Dishes 65

Crispy Chicken Wings 46–7
Crispy Fried Egg 192
Crispy Fried Garlic 172–3
Crispy Fried Shallots 174–5
Crispy King Prawns for Stir-fry
    Dishes 64
Crispy Pork Belly 33
Crispy Prawns in Sweet Chilli
    Tamarind Sauce 128–9
Crying Tiger Steak 126–7
cucumber
    Cucumber Relish 170
    Fresh Spring Rolls 23–4
    Grilled Chicken Salad 108–9
curries 83–92
    Beef Massaman Curry 86–7
    Chicken Jungle Curry 2,
        91–2
    Chicken Red Curry 84–5
    Green Curry 88–9
    Panang Pork Curry 90
curry pastes vi, 11
    Green Curry Paste 186–7
    Panang Curry Paste 184–5
    see also Massaman Curry
        Paste; Panang Curry Paste;
        Red Curry Paste

deep-frying 15–16
desserts
    Banana in Coconut Milk 197
    Chocolate and Banana
        Paratha 198
    Coconut Ice Cream 199
    Coconut Sticky Rice with
        Mango 195–6
    Fresh Fruit Salad 194

Mango Sorbet 201
Thai-style Banana Fritters
    200
dipping sauces
    Fermented Soybean Dipping
        Sauce 166
    Fish Sauce and Chillies 168
    Peanut Dipping Sauce 162
    Seafood Dipping Sauce 167
    Spicy Dipping Sauce 165
drinks
    Fruit Cooler 203
    Thai Iced Tea 202
Drunken Noodles 138–9

eggs v
    Beef Noodles 136–7
    Crispy Fried Egg 192
    Drunken Noodles 138–9
    Egg Fried Rice 145–6
    Prawn Pineapple Fried Rice
        154–5
    Stir-fried Noodles with Soy
        Sauce 134–5
    Thai Fried Noodles 132–3
    Thai-style Omelette 120–2
equipment 3–9
evaporated milk
    Prawn Hot and Sour Soup
        100–1
    Thai Iced Tea 202

fish
    Fish Cakes 56–7
    Steamed Sea Bass 130
fish sauce (nam pla) 12
    Fish Sauce and Chillies 168

Fruit Cooler 203
frying
  deep-frying 15–16
  stir-fry dishes 59–82

galangal 13–14
  Chicken Soup with Galangal
    102–3
  Green Curry Paste 186–7
  Massaman Curry Paste 181–3
  Panang Curry Paste 184–5
  Pork and Rice Soup 98–9
  Prawn Hot and Sour Soup
    100–1
  Red Curry Paste 179–80
  Tom Yum Style Fried Rice
    with Pork 158–9
garlic 14
  Crispy Fried Garlic 172–3
  Garlic in Oil 189–90
  Garlic and Pepper Prawns
    Stir-fry 76–7
ginger
  Chicken and Ginger Stir-fry
    78–9
  Chicken Over Rice 152–3
  Fermented Soybean Dipping
    Sauce 166
Glass Noodle Soup 96–7
green beans
  Chicken Jungle Curry 91–2
  Fish Cakes 56–7
  Papaya Salad 110–11
  Pork and Holy Basil Stir-fry
    80–1
Green Curry Paste 186–7
  Green Curry 88–9

jasmine rice vi, 12, 131
  Chicken Over Rice 152–3
  Chilli and Basil Fried Rice
    156–7
  Coconut Rice 147–9
  Egg Fried Rice 145–6
  fried rice 142–3, 147–8
  Pork and Rice Soup 98–9
  Prawn Pineapple Fried Rice
    154–5
  rice cooker method 142
  stovetop method 144
  Toasted Rice 178
  Tom Yum Style Fried Rice
    with Pork 158–9
juicer 3

lemongrass 14
lime juice 14
  Chicken Jungle Curry 91–2
  Chicken Soup with Galangal
    102–3
  Crying Tiger Steak 126–7
  Curry Chicken Noodle Soup
    104–5
  Fish Sauce and Chillies 168
  Fresh Fruit Salad 194
  Instant Noodle Salad 114–15
  Mango Sorbet 201
  Mixed Salad with Peanut
    Dressing 106–7
  Papaya Salad 110–11
  Pork and Rice Soup 98–9
  Pork Salad 112–13
  Prawn Hot and Sour Soup
    100–1
  Seafood Dipping Sauce 167

Spicy Dipping Sauce 165
Steamed Sea Bass 130
lime leaves 14

Mama's Crispy Volcano
    Chicken 2, 122–3
mangoes
  Coconut Sticky Rice with
      Mango 195–6
  Fruit Cooler 203
  Mango Sorbet 201
Massaman Curry Paste 181–3
  Beef Massaman Curry 86–7
  Curry Chicken Noodle Soup
      104–5
mint 14
Money Bags 28–9
mushrooms
  Beef and Oyster Sauce Stir-
      fry 68–9
  Cashew Chicken Stir-fry
      70–1
  Chicken Crispy Spring Rolls
      43–5
  Chicken Jungle Curry 91–2
  Chicken Soup with Galangal
      102–3
  Mixed Vegetables in Oyster
      Sauce 118–19
  Money Bags 28–9
  Mushroom Curry Puffs 26–7
  Prawn Hot and Sour Soup
      100–1
  Stir-fried Noodles 140–1
  Tom Yum Style Fried Rice
      with Pork 158–9
  Vegetable Spring Rolls 20–2

noodles 12, 131
  Beef Noodles 136–7
  Chicken Crispy Spring Rolls
      43–5
  Curry Chicken Noodle Soup
      104–5
  Drunken Noodles 138–9
  Fresh Spring Rolls 23–4
  Glass Noodle Soup 96–7
  Instant Noodle Salad 114–15
  Pork and Crispy Vegetable
      Spring Rolls 30–2
  Stir-fried Noodles 140–1
  Stir-fried Noodles with Soy
      Sauce 134–5
  Thai Fried Noodles (Pad
      Thai) 132–3
  Vegetable Spring Rolls 20–2
  Vermicelli Bean Thread
      Noodle Stir-fry 66–7
nuts *see* cashew nuts; peanuts

Omelette, Thai-style 120–2
oyster sauce 12
  Beef Noodles 136–7
  Beef and Oyster Sauce Stir-
      fry 68–9
  Cashew Chicken Stir-fry
      70–1
  Chicken Crispy Spring Rolls
      43–5
  Chicken and Ginger Stir-fry
      78–9
  Chicken and Prawn Toasts
      54–5
  Chilli and Basil Fried Rice
      156–7

Crispy Chicken Wings 46–7
Crispy Prawns in Sweet
  Chilli Tamarind Sauce
  128–9
Crying Tiger Steak 126–7
Dried Fried Pork 39–40
Drunken Noodles 138–9
Garlic and Pepper Prawns
  Stir-fry 76–7
Mama's Crispy Volcano
  Chicken 2, 122–3
Marinated Stir-fry Beef 61
Marinated Stir-fry Chicken
  Thighs 63
Marinated Stir-fry Pork 60
Mixed Vegetables in Oyster
  Sauce 118–19
Money Bags 28–9
Pork and Rice Soup 98–9
Pork Skewers 37–8
Pork and Vegetable Crispy
  Spring Rolls 30–2
Southern Thai-style Pork
  Belly Stew 93–4
Stir-fried Noodles 140–1
Stir-fried Noodles with Soy
  Sauce 134–5
Sweet and Sour Chicken Stir-
  fry 72–3
Thai-style Omelette 120–2
Tom Yum Style Fried Rice
  with Pork 158–9
Vegetable Spring Rolls
  20–2
Vermicelli Bean Thread
  Noodle Stir-fry 66–7

Pad Thai 131, 132–3
pak choi
  Beef Noodles 136–7
  Drunken Noodles 138–9
  Mama's Crispy Volcano
    Chicken 2, 122–3
  Stir-fried Noodles with Soy
    Sauce 134–5
Panang Curry Paste 184–5
  Panang Pork Curry 90
Papaya Salad 110–11
peanuts
  Dry Roasted Peanuts 177
  Mixed Salad with Peanut
    Dressing 106–7
  Panang Curry Paste 184–5
  Papaya Salad 110–11
  Peanut Dipping Sauce 162
  Thai Fried Noodles (Pad
    Thai) 132–3
peppers
  Beef and Oyster Sauce Stir-
    fry 68–9
  Cashew Chicken Stir-fry
    70–1
  Chicken and Ginger Stir-fry
    78–9
  Drunken Noodles 138–9
  Mixed Vegetables in Oyster
    Sauce 118–19
  Sweet and Sour Chicken Stir-
    fry 72–3
pestle and mortar 3
pineapple
  Chicken Pineapple Stir-fry
    74–5
  Fresh Fruit Salad 194

Fruit Cooler 203
Prawn Pineapple Fried Rice
    154–5
Sweet and Sour Chicken Stir-
    fry 72–3
pork
    Crispy Pork Belly 33
    Dried Fried Pork 39–40
    Instant Noodle Salad 114–15
    Marinated Stir-fry Pork 60
    Money Bags 28–9
    Northern Thai-style Sausage
        Meatballs 41–2
    Panang Pork Curry 90
    Pork and Holy Basil Stir-fry
        80–1
    Pork and Red Curry Stir-fry
        82
    Pork and Rice Soup 98–9
    Pork Salad 112–13
    Pork Skewers 37–8
    Pork and Vegetable Crispy
        Spring Rolls 30–2
    Salt and Chilli Pork Ribs
        34–6
    Southern Thai-style Pork
        Belly Stew 93–4
    Tom Yum Style Fried Rice
        with Pork 158–9
    Vermicelli Bean Thread
        Noodle Stir-fry 66–7
potatoes
    Beef Massaman Curry 86–7
    Mushroom Curry Puffs 26–7
prawns
    Chicken and Prawn Toasts
        54–5

Coconut Prawns 58
Crispy King Prawns for Stir-
    dry Dishes 64
Crispy Prawns in Sweet
    Chilli Tamarind Sauce
    128–9
Garlic and Pepper Prawns
    Stir-fry 76–7
Prawn Hot and Sour Soup
    100–1
Prawn Pineapple Fried Rice
    154–5
Thai Fried Noodles (Pad
    Thai) 132–3

Red Curry Paste 179–80
    Chicken Jungle Curry 91–2
    Chicken Red Curry 84–5
    Corn Fritters 18–19
    Crispy Chicken Wings 46–7
    Curry Chicken Noodle Soup
        104–5
    Fish Cakes 56–7
    Northern Thai-style Sausage
        Meatballs 41–2
    Peanut Dipping Sauce 162
    Pork and Red Curry Stir-fry
        82
rice *see* jasmine rice; sticky rice
rice cooker 3

salads 95
    Grilled Chicken Salad
        108–9
    Instant Noodle Salad 114–15
    Mixed Salad with Peanut
        Dressing 106–7

Papaya Salad 110–11
Pork Salad 112–13
Salt and Chilli Pork Ribs 34–6
Seafood Dipping Sauce 167
sesame seeds
    Chicken and Prawn Toasts 54–5
    Coconut Sticky Rice with Mango 195–6
    Thai-style Banana Fritters 200
shallots 14
shrimp, dried
    Fresh Fruit Salad 194
    Papaya Salad 110–11
shrimp paste
    Green Curry Paste 186–7
    Massaman Curry Paste 181–3
    Panang Curry Paste 184–5
    Red Curry Paste 179–80
skewers
    Chicken Satay 48–9
    Pork Skewers 37–8
soups 95
    Chicken Soup with Galangal 102–3
    Curry Chicken Noodle Soup 104–5
    Glass Noodle Soup 96–7
    Pork and Rice Soup 98–9
    Prawn Hot and Sour Soup 100–1
soy sauce v, 12
soybean paste: Fermented

Soybean Dipping Sauce 166
spices vi
    spice grinder 3
spring onions 14
spring rolls
    Chicken Crispy Spring Rolls 43–5
    Fresh Spring Rolls 23–4
    Pork and Crispy Vegetable Spring Rolls 30–2
    Vegetable Spring Rolls 20–2
sriracha sauce
    Chicken Pineapple Stir-fry 74–5
    Sweet and Sour Chicken Stir-fry 72–3
starters 17–58
Steamed Sea Bass 130
steamer 4
sticky rice 12, 131
    Coconut Sticky Rice with Mango 195–6
    Northern Thai-style Sausage Meatballs 41–2
    rice cooker method 150
    steamer method 151
    Toasted Rice 178
stir-fry dishes 59–82
store-cupboard ingredients 11–12
Sweet Chilli Sauce 169
    Chicken Pineapple Stir-fry 74–5
    Crispy Prawns in Sweet Chilli Tamarind Sauce 128–9

Mama's Crispy Volcano
   Chicken 2, 122–3
Mixed Salad with Peanut
   Dressing 106–7
Sweet Chilli Chicken Balls
   52–3
Sweet and Sour Chicken Stir-
   fry 72–3
Sweet and Sour Chicken Stir-
   fry 72–3
sweetcorn: Corn Fritters 18–19

Tamarind Paste 188
   Beef Massaman Curry 86–7
   Chicken Pineapple Stir-fry
      74–5
   Chilli Paste 163–4
   Crispy Prawns in Sweet
      Chilli Tamarind Sauce
      128–9
   Mama's Crispy Volcano
      Chicken 2, 122–3
   Peanut Dipping Sauce 162
   Prawn Hot and Sour Soup
      100–1
   Thai Fried Noodles (Pad
      Thai) 132–3
Tea, Thai Iced 202
Thai Fried Noodles (Pad Thai)
   132–3

Thai Iced Tea 202
Toasted Rice 178
   Pork Salad 112–13
tofu
   Fried Tofu 25
   Thai Fried Noodles (Pad
      Thai) 132–3
Tom Yum Style Fried Rice with
   Pork 158–9
tomatoes
   Chicken Pineapple Stir-fry
      74–5
   Chicken Soup with Galangal
      102–3
   Fresh Fruit Salad 194
   Grilled Chicken Salad 108–9
   Papaya Salad 110–11
   Prawn Hot and Sour Soup
      100–1
   Tom Yum Style Fried Rice
      with Pork 158–9

vegetable oils v
Vegetable Spring Rolls 20–2

wok 4–9
   carbon-steel 4–5
   cleaning 8–9
   seasoning 5–7
   using and caring for 7–8